*f*P

build your own garage

BLUEPRINTS AND TOOLS TO UNLEASH YOUR COMPANY'S HIDDEN CREATIVITY

Bernd H. Schmitt
and
Laura Brown

THE FREE PRESS

New York London Toronto Sydney Singapore

The Free Press
A Division of Simon & Schuster, Inc.
1230 Avenue of the Americas
New York, NY 10020

The authors gratefully acknowledge permission from the following sources
to reprint material in their control: Gail Anderson for all the illustrations and
photographs within *Build Your Own Garage,* copyright © 2001 by Gail Anderson.

THE FREE PRESS and colophon are trademarks of Simon & Schuster, Inc.

Designed by Brady McNamara

Manufactured in the United States of America

10 9 8 7 6 5 4 3 2 1

Library of Congress Cataloging-in-Publication Data
Schmitt, Bernd.
    Build your own garage : blueprints and tools to unleash your company's
    hidden creativity / Bernd H. Schmitt and Laura Brown.
        p. cm.
    Includes bibliographical references and index.
    1. Creative ability in business.   2. Technological innovations—Management.
3. Organizational learning.   I. Brown, Laura.   II. Title.
HD53 .S36 2001
658.5'14—dc21   2001031528

ISBN 0-7432-0260-0

This book is dedicated

SCHMITT: To Apollo and Dionysos, who taught me that creativity has many faces

Laura Brown: To my father, the late Justin W. Brown, who showed me that creativity is everywhere

CONTENTS

In the spring of 1999, I set up a Web site for my last book, *Experiential Marketing*. Under the icon "SCHMITT and his crew," the visitor found "The Garage," described as the "boiler pot of creative energy," and introduced with the following definition:

> Dictionary definition: A building or compartment of a building used for housing an automotive vehicle.

(Just cars? Or what else?)

> A place for projects. A place to put the outrageous, impractical things so that the rest of the house won't get messed up. A place where orderly people are uncomfortable.

(What house? What people?)

A crazy, iconoclast place where ideas are thriving and where websites and innovative projects are born. A place for lateral thinkers, where the sharp edge of intelligence is not blunted in endless meetings; where ideas can be born, nurtured and released into the world, all in the space of the same working day.

This passionate and exuberant posting was the beginning of my own thinking about The Garage. Soon after, I began talking about building The Garage in my speeches on "the dynamic brand-focused company" and "the experience-oriented organization." I finally fleshed out The Garage as a formal concept that represents the organizational spirit, structures, and processes of the type of organization that drives creativity and innovation. Out of that arose the need to share the idea with the business community at large in a book.

When I began working on the book, I soon realized that I did not want to write an ordinary business book. A book with concepts and war stories. A book with boxes and arrows. I wanted to write a book that brings together the structured and analytical with the spontaneous and passionate. A book that in its content and style reflects the creative and innovative nature of The Garage. I wanted to create a book that included business concepts, short stories, and funky photography. I wanted to link the book to a Web site that provides additional content, interaction, and video. In other words, I wanted to produce a multimedia product, and I didn't want to wait until I was senile to do it. This required that I ask other people for help.

First and foremost, I asked Laura Brown to be my co-author. I had worked with Laura Brown before, most notably on *Experiential Marketing,* where she appears as the enigmatic figure who asks the really tough questions at the end of each chapter. I asked her to write the short stories or "business parables" that I had envisioned for the beginning of the chapters. As usual, Laura's ultimate contribution went far beyond what I had imagined, and she has left her imprint throughout the book.

Both Laura and I then asked photographer and graphic artist Gail Anderson to do the iconographic photos for each business parable and to design all figures and graphics.

The Web site, www.BuildYourOwnGarage.com, was designed by

"SCHMITT and his crew," which included for this particular project David Myers and Daniel Ramirez.

A special thanks to the students of my Spring 2001 class on corporate creativity. They presented exciting and creative projects including projects on creative recruiting, a presaturated wiper for industrial usage, a Hollywood films fund, an entertainment magazine, the "Wall" at GE Capital, the "Ark" building in London, as well as a theater play on Dinasaur Inc. vs. Dionysos Inc. and on creative challenges in life.

There were other people who contributed to this book, knowingly and unknowingly, and I wish to thank them as well: Mindy Ji for sharing with me her insights on marketing and management theory; David Rogers for reading the entire manuscript and making critical suggestions on its terminology; and Karen Vrotsos for reading the manuscript and preparing several cases. I also wish to thank Mr. Robert Wallace, the editor of the book, and Cornelia Faifar at The Free Press. Special metaphysical greetings to Apollo and Dionysos to whom I have dedicated the book. Your presence will be felt throughout this book.

Enjoy *Build Your Own Garage.*

PREFACE BY LAURA BROWN

When SCHMITT suggested that I write a preface about the creation of the business parables in this book, I wasn't wild about the idea.

For one thing, I usually find it tedious when people discourse about their own creative process. Unless you're James Joyce or somebody like that, who cares? For another thing, writing about the creative process seemed a doomed idea from the start—creativity is ineffable, not a subject for analysis and discussion. Finally, I realized I was resisting the idea because I didn't exactly consider the parables my own creative work. They were the result of a collaborative process and hence not entirely mine. This last point made me think.

What struck me was that the same could be said about any creative project in a business setting—it would necessarily be a collaborative process. That, I thought, might be worth writing about.

In writing the parables, I faced a number of problems that I'm sure would look all too familiar to managers: not enough time, limited scope, worries about what the "market" would like. There was also another, more interesting challenge: too many cooks. Over the past two years there have been lots of creative people working in SCHMITT's Garage. All of them have been enthusiastic about the parables, and all of them have been more than happy to offer their unsolicited, unbridled, free-associative suggestions about what "should happen" or what would be "really cool."

SCHMITT was the worst. He came up with most of the main plot lines for the parables, except the vampire story. A couple of the stories are closely informed by his psychology. (And it was SCHMITT who insisted on the gratuitous sex scene in "I Lost My Business Plan in the Woods.") He has an amazingly generative mind and gets a lot more ideas than anyone really needs. My problem was trying to predict which of SCHMITT's ideas would bore him by the time his adrenaline rush had subsided and he had stopped pacing around the office waving his arms. Arm-waving is fun, but it's only part of the creative process. The other part is hard work, hammering out the details, trying to protect the integrity of the whole.

It seems to me that businesses face the same challenge in using creativity: staying receptive to divergent influences—ideas from employees, input from consultants, advice from business publications—while still trying to keep the thing in one piece. To use SCHMITT's phrase, it's a task of "capturing and managing chaos," and I hope this book will offer some guidance on the process.

During the course of this project, I've had a lot of arched eyebrows and wisecracks from friends about the subject of the book—"Corporate creativity, isn't that a contradiction in terms?" After a while I began to feel as though I was setting up a joke: I fed them the line, and they came back with the inevitable punch line. "Ha! Corporate creativity! *That's* an oxymoron!"

To be honest, I would have been inclined to agree with them, had I not remembered an incident from years ago that broadened my view of creativity. I was working on a job site for the construction company that my father ran. Before entering the construction business, Daddy had been a fine artist, a serious painter and an animator for Walter Lantz Studios. I never knew why he stopped painting, but I had always felt sad about it. One day he stopped by the trailer where I was working and started talking to the superintendent about a job he was getting ready to bid. It was a lab at CalTech, and the challenge was to build a structure that could safely contain radioactive materials. Grabbing a stray piece of paper, Daddy sketched the solution he had worked out. By dividing the structure in a particular way, and by pouring concrete continuously for twenty-four hours, the builders could make concrete walls with no seams. No seams, no leaks. I had never seen my father so enthusiastic. Suddenly I understood how he might have received the same kind of reward from his work as he had from his painting. It was a kind of artistry, too.

I would like to thank Gail Anderson, David Rogers, Michele Russell, and Karen Vrotsos for their helpful comments on early drafts of the parables. I would also like to thank Howard Hertz.

May all your creative collaborations be as much fun as this one has been!

THE GARAGE NURTURES CHAOS
THAT BEARS A DANCING STAR

In the beginning there was chaos. Business despised it. And to protect itself from chaos, it created rules and procedures.

But then came the Garage. It nurtured chaos and used its *bizz, buzz,* and *stuff* to create a dancing star.

The Garage became the envy of all organizations.

Excerpt from *Garage-sagaen,* Book I, verses 1–3, trans. Georg I. Skaander.

chaos
and the garage

One must nurture chaos inside oneself to give birth to a dancing star.
—Friedrich Nietzsche, *Thus Spoke Zarathustra*

Chaos is associated with the unorganized state of primordial matter before the creation of distinct and orderly forms. In The Garage, everyone is still connected with this primordial state of creation and inspiration. The Garage captures chaos. The Garage nurtures chaos that gives birth to a dancing star.

The Garage is about the constant flux of new ideas, new technologies that result in new products and services. Work in The Garage is fun, inspiring, immediate. It is something that everyone can be proud of and feel involved in. The Garage is a place where creativity and innovation are the highest priority; where bureaucracy is banished; and where ideas are implemented fast.

This garagelike mentality has frightened the ranks of corporate execu-

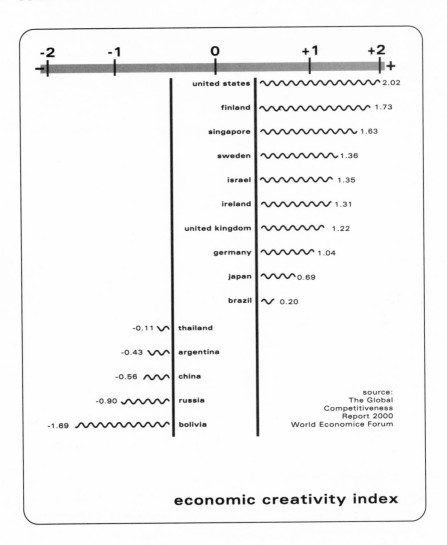

economic creativity index

tives, with their orderly empty desks at the corporate tower. For them, business is structure. They look at business as a rational venture. They indulge in formulating mission statements and strategies. They admire competencies and master plans. They are turned on by budgets and numbers. They want to rein in chaos through structures and procedures. Traditional business focuses on following procedures, not on generating new ideas; it focuses on the distant future, not on speed; it focuses on protection, not on sharing information. More generally, traditional business is tied to the status quo and not creating something new. As a result, things get done—rationally, mechanically, hierarchically—at a snail's pace.

At the same time, within the same ranks, there is a growing fascination with the innovative spirit of The Garage. Oh, if we could infuse passion into the rational nature of business-as-usual. If we could only marry chaos with structure. Big with small. Planning and control with entrepreneurship. If we could only be truly creative.

Tochi Yamada, head of R&D at Glaxo SmithKline, illustrates this paradox for the pharmaceutical industry. The *Financial Times* quotes him as saying, "We have to be big and small at the same time. I had to design something that would take advantage of scale. But we know for a fact that big can sometimes mean bad. So we had to design something that could also maintain agility and entrepreneurial spirit."[1] The same paradox also applies to Cisco. As the *Financial Times* observed, "Can a company that has doubled its payroll . . . maintain the entrepreneurial culture . . . ? Or, like IBM in the late 1970s, . . . is Cisco vulnerable to new and more nimble competitors?"[2]

CREATIVITY

To address this paradox, corporations need creativity, not just as an occasional exercise but as a force at the heart of the company. Corporations need to capture the spirit and focus of The Garage. They need to unleash hidden creativity. In fact, not only companies but entire countries and their governments need to be concerned about creativity. The Economic Creativity Index reported by the World Economic Forum for the first time in 2000 is closely related to economic growth. In 2000, the United States came out on top of the list, due to its pace-setting innovation, but it was closely followed by Finland and Singapore.

But creativity for what? Achieved by whom? Done how? What is creativity, anyway?

The *Encyclopaedia Britannica,* www.britannica.com, defines creativity as "the ability to make or otherwise bring into existence something new, whether a new solution to a problem, a new method or device, or a new artistic object or form." In their book *Corporate Creativity,* Alan G. Robinson and Sam Stern define corporate creativity as follows: "A company is

Knowledge—The Key Asset of the "Creative Economy"

In August 2000, *BusinessWeek* published a special double issue entitled "The 21st century Corporation." The lead article of the issue was entitled "The Creative Economy."

> Now the Industrial Economy is giving way to the Creative Economy, and corporations are at another crossroads. Attributes that made them ideal for the 20th century could cripple them in the 21st. So they will have to change, dramatically. . . . In the Creative Economy, the most important intellectual property isn't software or music or movies. It's the stuff inside employees' heads.

> "Ideas are capital. The rest is just money," states an ad by Deutsche Bank. However, because knowledge is intangible, it usually does not appear on the balance sheet. Consequently, the average market-to-book (M/B) ratio of the Standard & Poor 500 companies in the year 2000 exceeded 6.0. While this number may be too high (due to the inclusion of software and telecom companies, for example, which have lost market value), there are nonetheless tremendous knowledge values that do not show up on traditional balance sheets. Because of these developments, "accounting's 500-year exceptional durability is being severely tested" argues Baruch Lev, a professor at New York University and one of the leading proponents of a new accounting that focuses on "knowledge assets."

creative when its employees do something new and potentially useful without being directly shown or taught."[3]

So creativity is about "something new" and "useful." And that new thing can be just about anything in just about any sphere of human activity. In business terms, "creativity" can generate anything ranging from a small idea that improves a process or procedure to a radical new innovation. So it appears that creativity does not necessarily have to be a ground-breaking invention or a breakthrough in the way business is done. It does take innovation, however—that is, creativity made useful. And it needs to be original.

Webster's dictionary defines "original" as "of or relating to a rise or be-

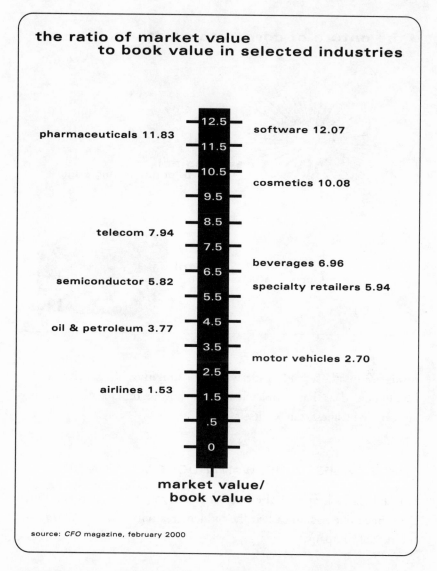

the ratio of market value to book value in selected industries

pharmaceuticals 11.83

software 12.07

cosmetics 10.08

telecom 7.94

beverages 6.96

semiconductor 5.82

specialty retailers 5.94

oil & petroleum 3.77

motor vehicles 2.70

airlines 1.53

12.5
11.5
10.5
9.5
8.5
7.5
6.5
5.5
4.5
3.5
2.5
1.5
.5
0

**market value/
book value**

source: *CFO* magazine, february 2000

ginning: Initial, primary, pristine." Creating something original means re-connecting with the chaos discussed earlier. We like the term *original* because it suggests tracing a concept back to its origin and then asking "what if?" about the assumptions that have grown up around the concept. The beauty of the term *original,* of course, is that it also describes products and ideas that are completely new. Webster's second definition of the word supports this meaning too: "taking independent rise: having sponta-

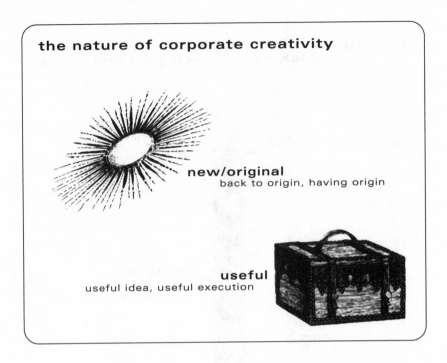

the nature of corporate creativity

new/original
back to origin, having origin

useful
useful idea, useful execution

neous origin: not secondary, derivative, or imitative." Creativity can also lead to new ideas that completely redefine how an organization can operate, can do business, can sell itself.

THREE CASES: BLUE, W, NTT DOCOMO'S I-MODE

Let's take a look at several examples of innovative products and initiatives. Each one has unleashed the hidden creativity of a fairly large and traditional company.

Blue

Blue is a new credit card launched by American Express in September 1999.[4] Ho-hum, you say, another AmEx card. Zzz.

But no! Blue is new; Blue is different. It starts with the name: "Blue." Not "the Blue Card," just "Blue." From the stodgy inventor of the Gold, Platinum, and Black cards comes an evocatively named credit card designed especially for the lifestyles of the young and Internet-savvy. The brand is positioned as "modern and hip—yet accessible" and "possessing confidence and a smart irreverence." In a market saturated with identical products, Blue stands out; within only six months of its launch, the new card was boasting more than a million cardholders, half of which were new American Express users.

So what is Blue? Blue offers all the features of the typical high-end credit card: no annual fee, a low annual percentage rate, a rewards program, and business accounts. But according to AmEx, Blue also has "stunning looks and brains too."

The brains, and creativity, come from the Smart Chip on every card: Blue is the first credit card to offer this feature. Right now this Smart Chip is giving Blue members added convenience and security for online transactions. By using an inexpensive SmartCard Reader, Blue shoppers can pay for online purchases with a simple swipe of the card. Special software enables Blue members to insert their cards into the Reader, go online, and pay with a single "Complete Purchase" button at the checkout of their favorite e-commerce site.

Okay, you say, the Internet purchase feature is neat, but is it really enough to justify the hoopla? Honestly, not yet. But Blue is still an exciting and important new offering, for two reasons: first, it positions itself as much more than a credit card—it sees itself as an embodiment of a new lifestyle and new values. Second, Blue is *designed* for the future. Its future potential is far more exciting than its present capacity: the Smart Chip can be updated to include as many other functions as can be imagined. According to AmEx, "no matter how fast the world changes, Blue will help you keep up." In fact, in June 2000, AmEx launched a contest among Java developers—with a first prize of $50,000—to find the most innovative new applications for Blue's Smart Chip. Who knows what they will have come up with by the time you are reading this book?

W

A division of Starwood Hotels, which also operates the Sheraton, the Westin, and the Luxury Collection, W is redefining the hotel experience for Generations X and Y.[5] W's plans include more than twenty hotels by the end of 2001 in key cities from New York and Los Angeles to Honolulu and Sydney.

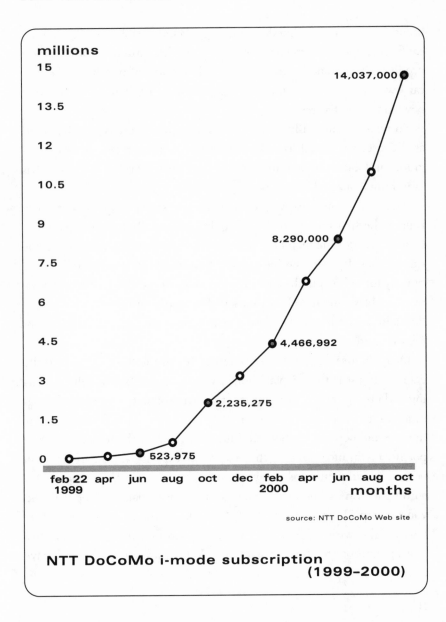

W represents a new and creative approach to hotels for the business traveler. Before W Hotels, people who traveled on business had severely limited choices in accommodations. There was the usual efficient-but-dull business hotel chain, like the Marriott, where every room looks the same and smells the same (have you ever noticed?). There was also the very expensive, typically traditional five-star hotel with its Louis XIV decor and arrogant staff. Despite acquisitions and refurbishments galore, the hospitality industry had not seen an original new brand launch in decades.

But now W has set out to define its own category in the hotel industry: "The much ballyhooed W brand incorporates the urban boutique concept popularized by design maven Ian Schrager, but also maintains an MTV-hip, New Age sophistication about it with an eye on attracting the laptop-toting, high-tech business traveler." How's that for a customer target definition?

Indeed, at the core of W's offering is an understanding and responsiveness to the customer that is surprising. The Internet generation want more than just a business hotel when they travel. They also want the experiences and amenities that have come to define their lifestyle. They don't want just a pool and a few weight machines—they want the first-rate health club facilities they have at home. They don't want just fast check-in—they want fast Internet connections. They don't want just promises of quality service—they want a different attitude in a hotel staff: down-to-earth, yet hip, and genuinely concerned with meeting their needs. And they want a cool bar; not surprisingly, W's food and beverage profit margins are 40–50 percent, which is very rare in the industry. At W, the employees wear black, in tune with the aesthetic of their customers, and are trained to answer the phone not by saying, "Room Service," or "Housekeeping," but by saying, "Whatever, whenever." Just as W's clientele is reshaping the norms of business, so W is reshaping our expectations of hotels.

NTT DoCoMo's i-mode

Let's switch gears now and take a look at a service that has become the envy of telecommunications providers worldwide.[6] The i-mode service offered by Japan's largest mobile telecommunications provider, NTT DoCoMo (formerly NTT Mobile Communications Network), was introduced on February 22, 1999. The service experienced rapid growth and surpassed 10 million users on August 6, 2000 and 20 million users in February 2001. Within two years, 15 percent of the Japanese population was using i-mode. More than tens of thousands of official Web sites and independent sites were available. Soon hundreds of companies provided information services through i-mode—sixty-seven firms had initially signed up.

DoCoMo's i-mode is a third generation mobile phone technology that provides continuous connection with the Internet via mobile phones. Personal users can access a wide range of interactive online services, including mobile banking for dozens of major banks, news and stock updates, telephone directory services, ticket reservations, online book sales, restaurants and karaoke information and booking, network games, and much more. Future business uses will include data exchange between sales managers and headquarters, streamlining the business operations of an enterprise. The service can also be used to exchange e-mails with computers, personal digital assistants, and cellular phones. The e-mail address is simply the cellular number followed by the DoCoMo URL, and e-mail is instantly displayed because i-mode is always on.

The i-mode system is also extremely attractive for Internet content providers (small or large) who simply add their fees to the subscribers' cellular phone bills collected by NTT DoCoMo. In 2000 DoCoMo collected 9 percent as a commission charge. For example, the Cybird Company, a small Japanese firm, has become highly profitable by offering more than fifty services to mobile users while discontinuing its unprofitable Internet site for personal computer users. One of the services charges 85,000 subscribers 300 yen a month for reporting the wave conditions on the Japanese coasts. Bandai Company, a toymaker and inventor of the Tamagotchi Virtual Pet, has signed up 1.3 million users to embellish their cell phones with screensaver images of popular musicians and cartoon characters.

NTT DoCoMo executives point out that a major reason for i-mode's success is its simplicity. Another reason is that it is a lifestyle product that is extremely popular among Japanese teenagers. To appeal to the target segment, NTT DoCoMo mobile phones look like toys and allow the display of several cartoon characters (Mitemite Kun, Monta, Pipi, Momo Chan, and others) on the i-mode terminal standby screen.

With Sony, NTT DoCoMO reached an agreement to combine i-mode and Playstation technologies. With Disney, NTT DoCoMo reached an agreement to provide a daily Disney character screen saver. With Dentsu,

Japan's largest advertising agency, NTT DoCoMo established an advertising agency for i-mode-based advertising.

As Elliott Hamilton, senior vice president at the Strategis Group, an e-data resources firm, noted: "Other wireless carriers, handset vendors, and software providers can look to i-mode as a successful benchmark to be emulated in their own country."

AN OVERVIEW OF THE FRAMEWORK OF THE BOOK

The Garage is the prototype of the creative organization. It is the spirit of The Garage that must resonate within the entire organization and shake it into action. As we have shown in Chapter 1, this spirit includes capturing, nurturing, and managing chaos to harness corporate creativity.

The figure shows the framework of corporate creativity used in this book. To build its own garage, the company needs three key elements and activities that make creativity work within it: *the bizz, the buzz,* and *the stuff*. These elements—and how they interact—will be discussed in detail in Chapter 2.

To create the right relation between *the bizz, the buzz* and *the stuff,* The Garage needs a broad-based mission about corporate creativity (or what we call "The Blueprint of The Garage") as well as specific implementation tools for infusing creativity into every project and initiative (or what we call "The Toolbox of The Garage"). In Chapter 3, we present both and show how the blueprint and the tools are used as essential strategy, recruiting, resource, and communication devices.

Moreover, The Garage needs organizational taskforces (or what we call "The Mastercrafts of The Garage") that work cross-functionally in bringing together *the bizz, the buzz,* and *the stuff*. Mastercrafts cut across organizational silos and departments (such as finance, accounting, legal, marketing) to plan and execute creative projects of the organization in line with its blueprints. Mastercrafting is not a set of rigid rules or procedures. Rather, it is an iterative creativity-optimizing process and a set of guidelines for channeling creativity in practical and effective directions.

We discuss the following three Mastercrafts. The Technology Mastercraft employs its skills and expertise to leverage technology cross-functionally for the purpose of harnessing corporate creativity (Chapter

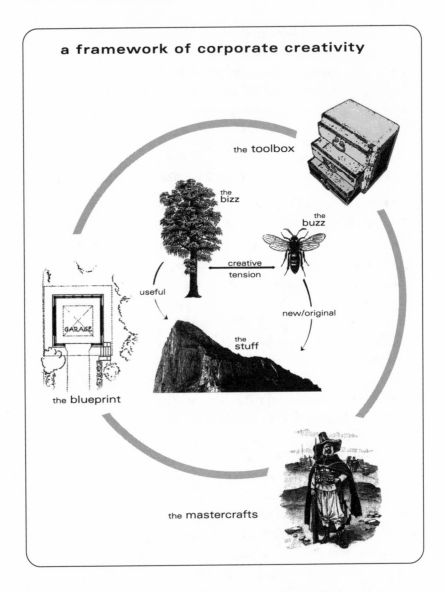

a framework of corporate creativity

the **toolbox**

the **bizz**

the **buzz**

creative tension

useful

new/original

the **stuff**

the **blueprint**

the **mastercrafts**

4). The Branding Mastercraft employs branding skills and expertise to make sure that the organization manages its branding initiatives and external and internal communications creatively (Chapter 5). The Mastercraft of Customer Experience Management is the science and art of managing the interface with customers in a creative way (Chapter 6).

Mastercrafts are indispensable creative forces of an organization. Without managing them appropriately, the organization does not harness all of its creative capabilities. Clearly there are other "crafts" in a business organization including finance, accounting, legal, marketing, and so on. They are important for the day-to-day functioning of an organization. And they do involve creativity—here and there. However, they are not *mastercrafts* because they do not manage the intersection between *the bizz, the buzz,* and *the stuff* and therefore do not leverage creativity and innovation across the entire organization. Unfortunately, most organizations have finance, accounting, legal, and marketing departments but lack these critical *Mastercraft* task forces.

Finally, in Chapter 7, we examine some of the key concepts of traditional management—mission, strategy, competence, implementation, and empowerment—and show how they need to be refocused to be valuable for corporate creativity.

HOW THIS BOOK WORKS

At the beginning of each chapter you will find a short story—or what we're calling a "business parable." A parable is a short fictitious story that illustrates a moral attitude or a religious principle. While our parables don't touch on moral or religious issues, they are meant to illustrate some important principles: in our case, principles about business.

Our parables are meant to be read partly for pleasure and partly for learning. Their purpose in the book is manifold—to illustrate some of the concepts to be discussed later in each chapter, to provoke thought and questioning, and, we hope, to engage the reader through enjoyment. All the stories are set in a business environment, and they all deal more or less explicitly with the business issues discussed further in each chapter. Every story is written in a different genre—you will find a vampire story, a love story, a murder story, a fairy tale, and a couple of interior monologues that may sound familiar to you. You will find characters that you may recognize: an idealistic consultant, a manager at a corporate retreat, a world-weary business traveler, a corporate vampire who exists only to suck the life out of his employees. Some of the settings will be familiar, too: a hot young start-up that's just been acquired by a corporate conglomerate; a company rebranding itself after a series of mergers; a firm struggling to keep in touch with its customer base; and the interior of a 747 aircraft.

With these stories, we hope to demonstrate a deeper point about creativity and human understanding—that is, that there is more than one way to convey ideas and more than one way to gain access to the spirit and the imagination. Business has traditionally limited itself to the world of the intellectual and the analytical, yet there is no reason that business should restrict itself to a single mode of communication and insight.

With this in mind, we have also commissioned photographer Gail Anderson to create photographic images for each of the parables. The visual is an extremely important mode for creativity and insight, and one that business has not used to its fullest potential. Human memory is largely a visual phenomenon: many of our memories come back to us as "snapshots" or visual markers of scenes we have experienced. For this reason, the photographs in the book focus on critical scenes and images that serve as icons for the parables' content.

The final component of the book is its Web site, www.BuildYourOwn Garage.com. On the site you will find updated information about the content of the book, added value in the form of various new content (including creativity tools and new cases of best practices), and more about business parables.

In sum, you are getting more than just a book: you are getting a multimedia experience of creativity. Enjoy.

CHAPTER TWO

entering the garage

What exactly is The Garage? How do we build The Garage? What happens in The Garage? How does The Garage capture, nurture, and manage chaos? And how can a garage affect a more traditional organization? Before we address these questions conceptually, we present our first parable, "They Walk Among Us." Modelled after Bram Stoker's novel *Dracula,* this parable contrasts the values of a young, successful, garagelike company with those of a horrific conglomerate monster.

"They Walk Among Us"

With apologies to Bram Stoker

Jonathan Harker's Journal

September 3.   Today the partners of Anglia, Ltd. spent our first day at our new parent company, LTVC—the Legendary Trans-V Corporation. The day began with something of a shock for us all—Mina, Lucy, Jack,

Today the partners of Anglia, Ltd.,
spent our first day at our new parent company,
the Legendary Trans-V Corporation

and I were most disappointed to learn that we would not be working together in the same office; indeed, we are not even to be situated on the
same floor. It will be a difficult adjustment for us, accustomed as we are to
working side by side. At least Mina and Lucy are to remain together and
continue their design work side by side—they work so harmoniously and
so well complement one another as to be almost two halves of the same
whole. Jack Seward, we have learned, will be working with LTVC's marketing people. I know my colleagues and I have enjoyed the rare advantage of close collaboration during our three years of independence, but
now with the buyout we must patiently suffer all the changes that will
doubtless come our way. We must have faith that the benefits of working
within so powerful a family of companies will outweigh any distress we
may feel. But I must confess, I do not wholly grasp LTVC's vision as yet.

I am not to be entirely alone in my work, however. It is a great honor
that the CEO of LTVC, Dean Calendula himself, will be working closely
with me during the transition period. He is a most striking-looking man,
tall and thin, quite pale, but with dark eyes and a full red mouth. His
dress is most distinctive, though a bit behind the fashion: a black suit with
a rich red tie and handkerchief.

This gentleman's elegant appearance is matched by his courtesy. His
praise for our little company and its achievements has been most gener-
ous, and I would suspect him of flattery were his manner not so sincere.
"Naturally we wish to learn all we can about how you have achieved your
fine success," he told me. "I hope it will not be an imposition if I sometimes pay you a call and observe your activities." I assured him that he was
most welcome in my office at any time.

Jack Seward's Journal

It seems that my life at LTVC will be little more than a stream of meetings, tightly scheduled and—as I believe—to no purpose. Dean Calendula has requested that I attend meetings that have but little relevance to
our business. An inauspicious beginning, to be sure, yet I hope that I may
soon be able to leave behind these endless planning and strategy meetings
and devote my energies to more productive work.

Mina Murray's Journal

Lucy and I are now settled comfortably in our new office, which commands a rare view of the harbor and of the buildings surrounding it. To have my brilliant and inquisitive partner Lucy with me is a great blessing, but I know that we will miss the society of Jack and Jonathan. Indeed, I fear that Lucy is already missing it more than she will acknowledge. She was gone from the office for over an hour this afternoon, and when she returned her manner was so quiet and abstracted that I could scarce believe she was the same girl. Never have I known Lucy to be so subdued. Perhaps this is her way of adjusting to our new surroundings, but I do hope she will be herself again soon.

Jonathan Harker's Journal

September 5.   I spent much of the day in conversation with Calendula, who continues to profess great interest in our accomplishments. During the afternoon, we met in Calendula's office. It is a tastefully decorated room, with an air of antiquity. His desk is an expansive mahogany piece, with nothing resting on it but an elegant MontBlanc pen set and a leather-bound organizer. I could not help but notice the absence of any photographs on his desk, but I expect that he must be a very private man. At the rear of the office, under the window, is a long, low mahogany chest that matches perfectly with the desk. When I made so bold as to admire the chest, Calendula smiled slightly and said only, "You are most kind. This piece belonged to my grandfather. I am very fortunate that my office is large enough to accommodate it."

Later in the afternoon, I believe I saw Lucy entering Calendula's office and shutting the door. I called out to her, but she did not hear me. I thought it odd that she did not stop to say hello after her meeting with Calendula, but no doubt she has many things to attend to, as do we all.

Shortly after five o'clock, I returned to Calendula's office to proffer some ideas for a new Romanian venture, but I found him already gone for the day.

Jack Seward's Journal

The meetings continue unabated. I am still not sure just *what* their purpose is meant to be. In the meanwhile, Calendula has been kind enough to lend me his own assistant while I familiarize myself with LTVC's marketing. Tall and almost ghostly pale, Renfield seems a bright young man, but prone to anxiety over details and preoccupied with counting and arranging things. When engaged in some task that I have set him, he performs his duties to the letter, but no further—his is not a mind that ranges to ask questions or to consider the reasons behind what he does. When he has nothing to do, he occupies himself with poring over office supply catalogues, comparing prices and quantities and making copious notes of the information he has gleaned. I have more than once observed him at his desk, his pale hand sweeping the blond hair off his blue-veined forehead, his lips moving silently as he ponders some question of numbers and quantities. At the end of the first week of our work together, he approached me and asked obsequiously if he might order a box of paperclips. When I consented, his strange young face brightened with a kind of supernatural light, and I thought he would never make an end of thanking me. While there is something endearingly innocent about this young man, I cannot help but wonder how I am to accomplish my work with none but he to assist me, particularly if I am to be detained in meetings for the greater part of each day.

Jonathan Harker's Journal

September 7.   Again I spent several hours in conference with Calendula. He shows particular interest in our technological innovations and what he calls our "method" of achieving them. I made an earnest effort to answer his questions, but I felt bound to point out that none of us believes that there has been any hard and fast method to the way we have worked. Quite simply, each of us has worked to the greatest of his abilities, inspired by a vision and determined to make it manifest—each with the same goal in mind and all with the spirit of adventure and comradeship. Calendula seemed genuinely puzzled and, I thought, a little impatient at my speech. To share with him a thing so near to my heart, only to be met with incomprehension, leaves me feeling most downcast.

Mina Murray's Journal

Lucy's distant and distracted manner has not faded; indeed, it has grown worse. Since our arrival at LTVC, she has not been the cheerfully irreverent girl that I used to know. She is more pale than usual, and when I inquire if she is well, she replies only that she is busy. She is in the habit now of leaving the office every afternoon—she will not tell me where she has been—and returning almost in a daze.

This morning I ventured a conversation with her, raising the question of the integration of our marketing strategy with that of LTVC—a problem that I am certain is vexing our dear Jack. Lucy regarded me with greater life in her eyes than I have seen since we joined LTVC, and exclaimed, "But my dear Mina, why should you concern yourself with that? You are a designer, not a marketer. Marketing is not part of your job description."

I confess I did not know how to reply to her. Since our early days of working together with Jack and Jonathan, we have relied on one another's insights and good judgment at all times. Naturally, each of us has special talents, but it has never been our way to limit our contributions according to our job descriptions. When I remonstrated with Lucy, she became distant and evasive once more, and I almost regretted having spoken out at all. My dear friend! I can only hope that time will bring her back to the vibrant young woman she once was.

Jonathan Harker's Journal

September 8.   A most disturbing incident has occurred. Yesterday, feeling a bit drowsy in the afternoon, I took a turn in the park opposite our building. It being a fine day, I spent a quarter of an hour resting on a stone bench, turning over and over in my mind a programming problem that had been puzzling me. No doubt as a result of the fresh air, a solution to my problem shortly presented itself to me. When I returned, I found Calendula walking out of my office. He did not speak but merely smiled mockingly. This morning when I arrived, I found a memorandum resting on my blotter. It was addressed generally to "Staff" and appeared to have been photocopied, as the print lay somewhat crookedly on the page. "All Staff members," it read, "are to remain at their desks and available at all times, except during authorized break times." It was signed at the bottom merely "C." I infer from this communication that Calendula is invoking some corporate regulation to punish me for my absence yesterday afternoon. I feel the walls of LTVC closing ever more tightly around me.

Jack Seward's Journal

Following his triumph with the paperclips, Renfield has each successive day asked me for permission to order some different item for his desk—a stapler, a box of staples, a notepad. Naturally, I have granted these simple requests, but I am mystified—I confess frustrated—by Renfield's peculiar behavior. I have noted that he keeps all in the most precise order on his desk and in his top drawer. This afternoon, he adopted a manner more than usually fawning and begged me for a Rolodex. When I pointed out to him that we have no need of a Rolodex, as we have all such information on our Palm organizers, his imploring look turned to one of rage. He fixed me with a glare that bespoke nothing short of murder. I marvel to think that I once considered him an innocent. An innocent, perhaps, but when thwarted in his desires, an innocent with the mind of a very madman! And yet his obsession with detail seems to be a common preoccupation with even the executives in this place. Between managing Renfield and attending the still-unstinting round of meetings, I feel that I have utterly lost myself, and I would be hard-pressed to say what value if any I am contributing to the company. I confess that I begin to have grave doubts about our acquisition by LTVC.

Jonathan Harker's Journal

There is something so strange about this place and all in it that I cannot but feel uneasy. I wish I were safe out of it, or that I had never come. Yet another restriction has been placed upon my personal freedom, as I have learned today that we are forbidden to use e-mail for any personal purposes whatsoever. The despair with which I received this news, coupled with the frustration of having no one to whom I could appeal, is difficult to express. The restriction is particularly distressing when I reflect that it was my forwarding of an e-mail joke to an acquaintance that initiated our contact with Interlink. It was principally the Interlink account, of course, that gave Anglia its great early success and began a series of partnerships that established our not inconsiderable reputation. It is with bitter irony that I now reflect that without that account we would certainly not be where we are now, housed—nay, imprisoned!—in LTVC.

Mina Murray's Journal

Alas! Poor dear Lucy is even worse than usual this morning. Indeed, when she arrived, I found her so changed that I hardly recognized her. She is morbidly pale, and came to work wearing a high-necked pink blouse and navy blue tailored trousers. In all the years that I have worked alongside Lucy, I have hardly known her to wear anything but black. Seeing her in this strange outfit, I hardly knew what to say. Indeed, it was all I could do to restrain myself from shaking her until she regained her senses. In this strange office, I cannot approach her with our old intimacy and directness. Quietly I asked her where her new clothes had come from. Smiling just a bit, like a shy little girl with a new treasure, she replied softly, "The Talbot's catalogue. I got a robin's-egg blue blouse just like this one, too. And pearl studs on sale."

The rest of the morning passed quietly. When I returned from lunch, I found Lucy gone. On her desk, however, I observed several memos and a purchase order specifying that a Pentium III computer be acquired for our office. I cannot imagine the purpose behind this, as designers have no use whatsoever for such a computer; our work has always been done on Apple computers, which are far better suited for such tasks. And yet there was the purchase order, signed by Dean Calendula himself. I am afraid these are mysteries beyond my ken.

Jonathan Harker's Journal

October 1.   I must put down everything exactly as it happened. Confined as I am within the building, with no e-mail access to friends or outside world, I left my office in a fit of restlessness and roamed the building itself. Stumbling upon the freight elevator, I began to climb the darkened, dusty staircase that winds around the elevator shaft. Old worn marble steps and the stale scent of cigarette smoke invoked a sense of time past, and at least I felt some respite from the artificial environs of my office. Between the sixth and seventh floors, I believe, I came upon a small and irregular-looking door. Driven by an irresistable curiosity, I tried this door. It was unlocked but stiff, and it took the full weight of my body to force it open.

Once through the door, I came upon what appeared to be a storage

I began to climb the darkened, dusty staircase
that winds around the elevator shaft. Old worn marble
steps and the stale scent of cigarette smoke invoked
a sense of time past ...

area. A thick layer of dust overlay everything in view. Relics of time past lay on old desks and typewriter stands ranged around the room: an ancient IBM Selectric, sheets of carbon paper, a large and cumbersome Dictaphone. A mechanical adding machine, such as I have not seen in many a year, rested atop a pile of faded memorandum forms. A pair of coffee mugs, on which I could barely make out the words *"excellence"* and *"teamwork,"* sat beside a box of IBM punch cards. I allowed my imagination to roam, thinking of the secretaries who perhaps sat at these very desks, eating doughnuts and using these very machines, typing and retyping memos, letters, and reports.

At the far side of the room were large windows that opened to the south and west of the building. Even through the thick dust, a warm and pleasant light streamed in. Looking around, I espied an old vinyl-covered couch, such as might have once stood in a reception area. Leaving my footprints in the dust as I went, I dragged the couch under the window so that I might enjoy the exquisite light. Caring not at all for the dust, I lay down.

I suppose I must have fallen asleep. I hope so, but what then transpired was so terrifyingly real that I cannot imagine it to be a mere dream. Suddenly I was not alone. Three beautiful young women slowly approached me. Although they stood in the slanting golden sun of the afternoon, they cast no shadow on the dusty floor. They stood for a long time looking at me and whispering among themselves. One held in her long white fingers LTVC's 1979 annual report. Another, wearing a business suit with white socks and Reeboks, clutched a datebook tightly to her bosom. Between these two stood a tall blond woman in a low-cut dress, her full red lips slightly parted. Falling from her sleeves and trailing in great flowing waves behind her were duplicate forms, pink, gold, yellow, green, in seemingly endless quantity. I was repulsed beyond description, and yet at the same time irresistibly drawn to the women. At length, the one in the business suit turned to the blonde and said firmly, "Yours is the right."

The woman then approached me, coy and yet somehow lascivious, the multicolored duplicate forms trailing behind her. She stood still for a moment, then leaned over me excruciatingly slowly. The papers, seemingly moving of their own free will, entwined themselves around and around my body. Their touch was like the touch of inhuman hands. The soft

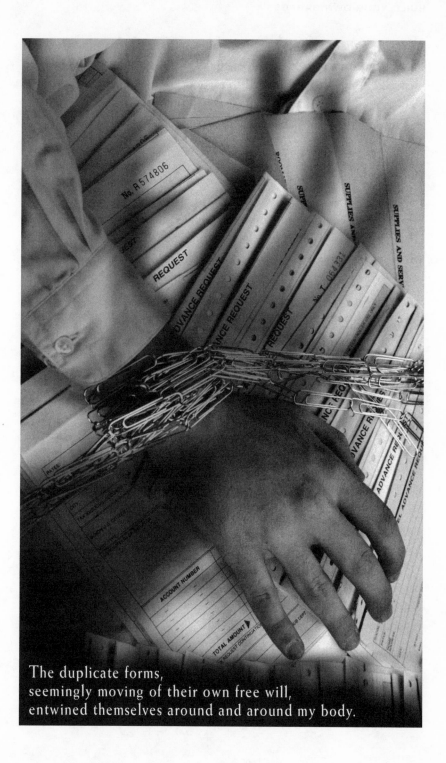

The duplicate forms,
seemingly moving of their own free will,
entwined themselves around and around my body.

rustling of the papers merged with the sound of the woman's gentle breathing coming closer and closer to my face. The skin on my neck tingled with anticipation. I longed to scream and flee from her, and yet I could not move. I lay back, helpless, in voluptuous anticipation.

Then in an instant Calendula appeared, seemingly out of the very dust of the air. A look of terrifying malignity glowed in his eyes. Seizing the woman nearest to me, he flung her away violently and roared, "How dare you touch him—any of you? How dare you cast eyes on him when I have forbidden it? Back, back, I tell you, all. This man is mine. There are ideas to be drained, energy to be tapped! There will be time enough for you later." The three women retreated, laughing and clinging to each other, with many a glance cast back at me over their shoulders. I must have lost consciousness; and when I awoke, I found myself again at my own computer. The hour was past five, and Calendula was nowhere to be seen. The office has become a sort of sanctuary, for nothing can be worse than those dreadful women who were—who *are*—waiting to suck my blood.

Jack Seward's Journal

I believe now that Renfield has entirely gone mad. He has been restless and distracted, interested in neither his accounts nor his office supplies. All morning he kept sighing and turning sharply around in his swivel chair. Then at midday he turned abruptly to me and cried, "You must take her away. You must not allow her to stay here!" Believing him undone, I tried to comfort him, but my kind words only inflamed him more. Almost weeping, he exclaimed, "If you knew what I risked in speaking to you, you would value my words at a higher price. O, take her away, I implore you! Take her away—before it is too late!"

And before I could speak a word, he bolted out of the office, a hail of paperclips flying from his desk and scattering on the floor. I have not seen him again this afternoon. I will make a note to speak to Calendula about it when my meetings are finished today.

E-mail Message from Mina Murray to Jack Seward

My dear Jack, I must share with you my alarm about our darling Lucy. She has not been herself since we joined LTVC. I have not wished to worry you or Jonathan and have hoped that she would regain her usual good spirits on her own, but I must now tell you that she has lost much of her energy and happiness. That her work has suffered terribly, there is no doubt—yesterday I observed her decorating an invitation with clip art. This afternoon there has been an even more frightening incident, and I can no longer keep my fears to myself. Returning from a trip to the ladies' room, I found Lucy leaning upon the window frame, tugging with all her strength in a vain attempt to open the window. Outside on the windowsill stood an enormous pigeon. I shudder to write these words, Jack, but it appeared that poor Lucy was trying to let the pigeon in. As I pulled her away from the window, she became distracted, casting her eyes here and there, and said in an awed voice, "His red eyes again." I stepped quickly to the window, waving my arms wildly to frighten the pigeon away. The bird's response was most unnerving. It fixed me with a malevolent stare that bespoke an evil intelligence, then slowly and deliberately spread its wings and flew away. Its piercing eyes were indeed red, a reflection, I must believe, of the early sunset. When I turned back to Lucy, I found her studying an office supply catalogue. I know not what these strange portents may mean, Jack, but I fear desperately for Lucy and I fervently hope that you may find a way to help us.

Jack Seward's Journal

I have written to my old friend and mentor, Abe Van Helsing, about the horror which Mina described and about the strange goings-on which we have all observed since our company was acquired by LTVC. Van Helsing was my org theory professor at Harvard Business School and has offered unfailing support since then. I believe it will take a mind of his caliber—nothing less than brilliant—to solve this mystery. For I am now convinced that everything we have observed is somehow related. Perhaps I have been rendered irrational by this week's round of sales meetings, yet I feel sure now that Renfield's strange warning was about Lucy. Lucy is in some kind of grave danger, as are we all. From what, I do not know, but I pray that Van Helsing may be able to uncover the dark secrets of LTVC.

E-mail from Abe Van Helsing to Jack Seward

My Dear Jack,

I am already on my way to you. Can it be true? Have I been naive in thinking it a mere legend? I must have more evidence before I reach such a conclusion. I will be with you soon.

I will wish to meet with you and your colleagues, and I must insist that we meet only *after five o'clock*. Bear with me, my dear boy, for if my suspicions are correct, this is the only time we can be completely safe. I trust you will make the arrangements.

AVH

Mina Murray's Journal

I fear I can no longer leave Lucy on her own. This morning I found her on hands and knees, disconnecting the wires running from her computer. When I asked her what she was doing, she replied in a quiet but frantic voice, "We must remove this machine." I made so bold as to remind her that it was her beloved Apple G4, the fastest processor in existence and the ideal machine for graphics work. "No matter!" she cried, her eyes rolling wildly. "It is not compatible! It cannot be networked! I must have a PC! I must run Windows! I cannot bear it any longer!" I fear she was simply raving, as any child knows that an Apple can be networked and that Apple products have long been compatible with others. It is a kind of madness I have heard of in others, but I never dreamed I would see it in one who was once so wise and so sensitive. Alas. I must put my trust in Jack to find a remedy, if one is to be found. When did I become so faltering and unsure? I used to think of Jack as my peer, and now, how distant he seems, though he is only upstairs.

Jonathan Harker's Journal

We have had a most shocking interview with Jack's former professor, Van Helsing. I must write it bluntly, for otherwise I will be overcome again with disbelief: Van Helsing suspects that Calendula is one of the Corporate Undead. Indeed, I have heard of such creatures but have never given much credence to these stories. Yet Van Helsing's description fits Calendula perfectly. He exists only to suck the lifeblood and creativity out of his employees. He is seen only between the hours of nine and five. And according to Van Helsing, if we do not soon take action, we shall be left like Jack's assistant Renfield—unable to think about anything but details. Or, I shudder to think, like those women whom I encountered in the storage area. There is one hope that Van Helsing shared:

> Your corporate vampire cannot bear to be in the same room with an Apple computer. It is anathema to him. Hitherto, Miss Mina, the G4 has been the greatest protection your dear Lucy has had. The vampire was unable to enter your office, which is why poor Lucy has been visiting his office upstairs. It is also why she was attempting to open the window when he was in pigeon form. You look surprised? Yes, the corporate vampire can take many different shapes to suit his purpose. In any case, Calendula could not have entered the room in any form as long as the Apple was in that room. If Miss Lucy should succeed in removing the Apples from their office, it will allow Nosferatu free access. It is fortunate for us, however, that LTVC must move as slowly as it does. Being the Corporate Undead, it will certainly take weeks, if not months, for its financial offices to process the purchase order and obtain the Pentium. But we must act and act soon, or poor Lucy is lost.

I know now that the chest in Calendula's office is a coffin. When I think of the three horrid women I encountered in the storage room, and imagine Lucy as one of them, I am overcome with horror. I pray that we shall be able to prevent this unthinkable disaster!

Mina Murray's Journal

Dr. Van Helsing has outlined a bold plan for us:

> We must hold Calendula in his office until the clock strikes five and even beyond. The Corporate Undead, being not alive, cannot act but between the hours of 9 and 5. To keep him in the place of work beyond his usual time means certain death for him. You must, together, conceive a plan to detain him. The success of your collaboration at

Yes, the corporate vampire can take many shapes
to suit his purpose.

present is a matter of life and death, not just for dear Lucy but for all of you and perhaps for many more.

I only hope that we still have the heart for such bold, concerted action.

Jonathan Harker's Journal

Our plans move on apace. Jack Seward is to arrange for Calendula to be detained in a meeting at the end of the day, and keep him away from his office and coffin as near to 5 o'clock as possible. My part in the plan has been to sabotage the projector on which the PowerPoint presentation is to be shown. I assured Van Helsing that to cause a disruption would be simple in the extreme, indeed, that such a malfunction was likely to occur even without my intervention. In the meanwhile, Mina is to hold Lucy by promising that the Pentium is scheduled to be installed.

Mina Murray's Journal

I found Lucy in Calendula's office at ten to five, just as Jack and Jonathan arrived. She became distraught upon seeing us all together. Fretfully, she cried, "But you don't have an appointment! See, here is his calendar!" Clutching the leather-bound datebook to her prim, pink collar, she fell, fainting, onto the plush carpet.

"We must let her sleep, so that we can act," urged Jack.

I turned to him. "But how to get rid of his coffin?"

"Pitch it out the window!" cried Jonathan.

"The window doesn't open," said Van Helsing. "It is sealed!"

"Of course," groaned Jack. "The windows of corporate towers cannot be opened. We should have thought of that!"

"No matter," cried Van Helsing, "we must break the glass. It is the only way." With that the brave doctor seized Calendula's Corporate Achievement Award—a grotesque mass of crystal and metal and dark wood— and threw it with all his might against the glass. The pane shattered, and the wind rushed in with a great sucking sound as though the office had never felt fresh air. The men lost no time in pushing out the remaining shards. Then to the task of raising the coffin. It was supernaturally heavy and seemed impossible to lift. "Just as I thought!" cried Jonathan in an instant. "It's anchored to the floor. It is corporate property." And indeed it was affixed with a cable and labeled with a small bar code. Fortunately, Jonathan had had the foresight to steal a pair of cable cutters from the Operations Office, and he freed the coffin with a few deft snips.

But perhaps we were too late! Outside the office came the ring of the elevator reaching the floor and the sound of the doors sliding open. Rapid steps approached and Calendula burst into the room.

"What are you doing?" he raged, in a voice that shook the building to its very foundations. "You pathetic fools! Do you think you can defy me? The Corporate Undead have walked these halls for generations—and halls all over the world." He lunged at the men, who were still struggling with the heavy coffin.

Little thinking what I did, I threw myself in the monster's path and held up the mouse from my Apple computer, which I had brought with me, having learned of its power from Dr. Van Helsing. At the sight of this symbol, Calendula snarled like an animal and recoiled in horror. His eyes blazed red, and his teeth glinted. With a grip of superhuman strength, he took me by the wrist and threw me across the room. The delay I had caused, however, gave the men the time they needed, and they pushed the coffin out the window. It plummeted to the street below.

Upon seeing his only sanctuary destroyed, Calendula turned on us with a look of indescribable rage and hatred, a malevolence that his polite veneer had hitherto concealed. Suddenly he seemed to become larger, and we shrank away in horror. I confess I wondered in that moment if we were equal to the task we had undertaken, so frightened was I for myself and the others. Calendula began to move toward us and we to retreat to the door, when suddenly the clock on the Acme Tower next door began to chime five.

Spinning 'round, the Thing writhed; and a hideous, blood-curdling screech came from the opened red lips. The body shook and quivered and twisted in wild contortions; the sharp white teeth champed together till the lips were cut and the mouth was smeared with a crimson foam. Then, before our unbelieving eyes, occurred a transformation so dreadful that I shall never forget it, no matter how long I may live. His screams subsiding, Calendula began to age horribly, the lines on his face deepening and the flesh shrinking and stretching tight over his skull. As the Thing dissipated, a cracked and disembodied voice—a sound straight from Hell—

As the Thing dissipated, a cracked and disembodied voice ... hissed the sacred words of the corporate credo: *mission, strategy, competence, implementation, empowerment.*

hissed the sacred words of the corporate creed: "Mission, strategy, competence, implementation, empowerment." And then It was gone. In an instant Calendula was reduced to nothing more than a pile of dust on the swivel chair behind his desk.

We looked on in horror, none of us able to speak. Suddenly, as one, we remembered Lucy. We had a moment of terrible speculation as we all knelt by her limp form. At length we revived her, and as she breathed, the color in her face slowly returned and she began to stir. Her eyes fluttered open, and I dared to think that I saw in them the same life energy that I had known before—dimmed by the exhaustion of her ordeal, but nevertheless the spark of the Lucy I had once known and loved. Her hand reached up to her neck and groped at her pink frilled collar and the short strand of pearls that surrounded it, and she gasped, "What the hell am I wearing?"

It was then that we knew that our Lucy had been returned to us and that by the grace of God her sweet life had been spared the evil of the Corporate Undead.

Jonathan Harker's Journal

Of this strange tale there remains only to tell the aftermath. We left Van Helsing and Mina with Lucy to discuss the Harvard case that Van Helsing was already planning to write, and Jack and I undertook to make a survey of the LTVC building. On every floor were the signs of death—death long overdue and for that all the more horrible. In cubicle after cubicle we found nothing but piles of dust where once there had been living beings—or rather, what had seemed living beings to us. Illusions all! All minions of Calendula, or more properly his victims. To think that we worked for weeks among the very living dead! And I still shudder at the thought that had we not acted when we did, had not Professor Van Helsing helped us recognize the monster for what he truly was, our beloved Lucy would surely have become one of them. And after her, would any of us have survived long?

Jack was deeply affected by these horrid sights, and turned to me with a look of misery on his face. His voice took on a tone of dread as he murmured, "We must return to my office." With a morbid apprehension, I accompanied him. There on a chair in front of a tidy desk was a small pile of dust. "Dear God!" cried Jack. "This was my assistant. This was Renfield. I would not have thought one so young . . ." His voice broke in sorrow. "And yet I knew. The pity of it, Jonathan, is that he tried to warn me about Calendula, about his designs on Lucy. I wonder if there was any way I could have helped him. . . ."

Ours was a narrow escape from the grip of the corporate vampire. Now, as the four of us work together on planning our next venture, we are reminded again and again of our great good fortune in escaping from the tomb of the legendary LTVC Corporation. Yet we cannot help but wonder how many others like Calendula there may be throughout the world and how many of the Corporate Undead walk among us still . . .

WHAT DOES THE BUSINESS PARABLE MEAN?

The strictures of traditional corporate culture are enough to suck the life energy out of anyone. Among the first forces to surrender is creativity, as personified in our parable by the designer Lucy who is so nearly lost to the Corporate Undead. The phenomenon of Corporate Vampirism spreads insidiously, creeping through organizations and destroying everything in its path. But through their stifling hierarchies, sterile interaction, and stultifying processes, the corporate bloodsuckers are also lining their own coffins. Ultimately, the suffocating institutions of the Corporate Undead will be defeated by a more innovative way of doing business, which may arise from external pressure (as in this parable) or may spring up from within the company itself.

A MODEL OF CORPORATE CREATIVITY

In this chapter, we look closely at The Garage as a model of corporate creativity: the organization best suited to harness corporate creativity and thus guarantee longterm market success. Garage. We will describe what makes up The Garage, including its business attitude and its sense of excitement. What's more, we will look at the three key components of The Garage: *the bizz, the buzz,* and *the stuff.* Finally, we will examine the suboptimal organizations that underperform in the area of creativity.

If the "New Economy" has taught us anything of lasting value in an organizational sense, it is that "old economy" companies need to be able to accelerate their change agenda. Today, environmental change occurs with frightening speed. This new and blinding rate of speed requires that organizations do more than simply "adapt." Nor do they need just to "learn." Adaptation and learning are important, but taken on their own, they are not enough. In today's business climate, the challenge is much greater, requiring initiative and invention. What companies really must do is to capture and manage creativity and keep the fresh and innovative spirit of The Garage, even as their operations grow and develop.

General Electric

A company that has lived the innovative spirit of The Garage for the last two decades—under the leadership of its legendary CEO Jack Welch—is General Electric (GE). Welch pushed through numerous radical changes at a company that was long known for being slow and stodgy. These initiatives resulted in a market capitalization of about $500 billion by the beginning of the new century and 100 quarters of uninterrupted growth in net income.

- Welch insisted that managers push their products into No. 1 or No. 2 positions—or else exit the business. This demand for market dominance required innovative thinking and product launches in many mature markets.
- Welch realized that creative ideas do not come only from the boardroom but from anywhere in a company. Thus, he created a culture and techniques (such as the GE Workout Sessions) that encouraged creative ideas and best practice sharing from line workers all the way up to top management.
- Welch inspired continuous change. To explore the opportunities of the internet age, he asked for Internet business blueprints that would intentionally destroy existing businesses.

Another company that has embarked on an ambitious initiative and has in fact started a crusade to recapture the innovative spirit of its own "garage" is Hewlett-Packard. The outcome of this endeavor at this point is unknown and depends on its exact implementation. Yet, what would have been the alternative? We don't have to look very far; we just need to cite the spectacular downfall of Xerox, whose stock in early 2001 traded at the same level as in 1961.

Hewlett-Packard

In November 1999, Hewlett-Packard (HP) started an initiative—internally and externally—built around the theme "Invent."[7] Carly Fiorina, who had become HP's president and CEO in July 1999, appeared in the initial spot standing next to a replica of the fabled garage where the company was born. The point of the campaign? To reconnect the company with the innovativeness that had made Hewlett-Packard a great company and to recreate a sense of entrepreneurship and vitality.

On the company's Web site, Ms. Fiorina posted the following promises:

> At HP, we're hard at work reinventing our company. We're going back to our roots of invention, to our radical beginnings in the original HP garage. Our goal is to unleash the vast talent and creativity within HP for one reason: so we can serve you better. . . . We promise to make your total customer experience with HP the best in the industry.

Fiorina began talking about "the Renaissance phase of the Information Age, where creativity and ideas are the new currency" and where "invention is a primary value." She stressed how "reinvention" had replaced "restructuring" and even "reengineering." She sketched the three intersecting vectors of appliances, infrastructure, and e-services through which HP must create value. She urged HP's partners and customers to be more inventive themselves and to reinvent their own businesses in "very fundamental ways."

Most important, Fiorina laid out the "rules of the garage"—the culture, way of thinking and behaviors that drive HP:

> Believe you can change the world, work quickly, keep the tools unlocked, work whenever, know when to work alone and when to work together; share tools, ideas, trust your colleagues. No politics, no bureaucracy: these are ridiculous in a garage. The customer defines a job well done. Radical ideas are not bad ideas. Invent different ways of working. Make a contribution every day. If it doesn't contribute, it doesn't leave the garage. Believe that together, we can do anything. Invent.

THE BIZZ, THE BUZZ, AND THE STUFF

Conceptually, the notion of The Garage developed in this book builds on the final chapter of SCHMITT's last book, *Experiential Marketing: How to Get Customers to Sense, Feel, Think, Act and Relate to Your Company and Brands.* The chapter, entitled "The Experience-Oriented Organization," contrasted two types of organizations: the Apollonian and the Dionysian organization. The terms *Apollonian* and *Dionysian* are associated with Greek mythology. *Apollonian* is related to the Greek god Apollo and signifies the measured, the ordered, the structured, and the rational. *Dionysian* is connected with the god Dionysos, and stands for the passionate, the ecstatic, the unbounded, and irrational:

> Applying the terms to present-day organizations, we can contrast as ideal types the Apollonian and the Dionysian organization. The Apollonian organization is of rational nature: harmonious, ordered, and planned. It is, ultimately, the result of the spirit of the enlightenment. The Dionysian organization is born out of a different understanding of reality. The Dionysian organization is of a passionate-creative nature; it thrives on chaos. (p. 236)

SCHMITT went on to argue that the experience-oriented organization needs both: planning, management, and measurement as well as excitement, initiative, and fun. In this book, we use the term The Garage for the type of organization in which both these elements come together. We have coined the term *the bizz* for a set of well-organized and structured activities resulting from the Apollonian spirit; we use the term *the buzz* for the motivation, passion, and excitement resulting from the Dionysian spirit. In The Garage there is always a creative tension between *the bizz* and *the buzz.* It is this tension that nurtures and captures chaos and transforms it into something highly creative (original and useful).

Moreover, The Garage is also extremely competent in running its day-to-day operations. It has the right facilities, the knowledge and research skills, and time-tested processes that make the operation run smoothly: This is what we call *the stuff.* In The Garage, facilities, knowledge, and skills are engaged in a useful and original fashion; they are

"What if we're still doing this when we're fifty?": A Dionysian Rebellion Against the Apollonian Organization

The 1999 20th-Century Fox comedy *Office Space* has become a huge cult success among college students. Written and directed by Mike Judge, the director of *Beavis and Butt-Head Do America,* and the creator of the *Milton* animated shorts, *Office Space* tells the story of a group of disaffected young programmers working for an enormous and faceless organization somewhere in the United States. The picture it paints of everyday worklife is comical but bleakly accurate: people sitting in rows of tiny cubicles, inept middle managers obsessed with paperwork, jobs reduced to mindless and endless rote tasks. The film makes hay of all the office inanities that are unfortunately as familiar as breathing: the photocopier that chronically jams, the computers that constantly hang, the co-workers who make noise, the bosses who are enamored of the latest business jargon words—all the little things that would bother us a lot less if our work were rewarding or engaging. When the bosses bring in "efficiency experts" to recommend layoffs, the main character tells them the truth about his approach to working: "It's not that I'm lazy, it's that I just don't care. . . . Fear of losing your job makes you work just hard enough not to get fired."

This film has figured out what's wrong with the way many of us work: "Human beings were not meant to sit in little cubicles staring at computer screens all day, filling out forms and listening to eight different bosses drone on about mission statements." After an elaborate plot to defraud the company ends, literally, in a burst of flame, the protagonist resigns and finds happiness as a construction worker.

The Dionysian rebellion against the Apollonian organization is affecting companies in other nations as well. "Years ago, Mitsubishi or other big companies were very solid, unshakable. But not anymore," says Japanese writer Haruki Murakami. "Young people these days don't trust anything at all. They want to be free. This system, our society, they won't accept such people."[8] Murakami has provided a very accurate portrayal of this new attitude in his award-winning novel *The Wind-up Bird Chronicle*—a must-read for any executive.

the result of a creative resolution of the tension between *the bizz* and *the buzz*.

Before we analyze the creative tension between *the bizz* and *the buzz,* let's first define these three key terms—*the bizz, the buzz,* and the *stuff*— more precisely.

the bizz

We will use the term *the bizz* to refer to the "tree of business knowledge"—including fundamental rules and proven procedures and principles of management action.

The bizz is Apollonian in nature. *the bizz* is about strategy and planning, structure and order. The basic orientation is that of control: controlling nature (and exploiting it via technology); controlling people through the use of power and incentives; and controlling actions via strategizing and planning over the course of time. The word *control* may sound oppressive. It is not meant to. Control implies reliability and security, and without some degree of that individuals often feel lost. Control and rules clear the path for creative initiative. In chapter 3 we offer the Three Creative Exploration Tools that provide the structure for creative management.

Without *the bizz,* creativity cannot result in something useful. Without *the bizz,* we will not be able to add value for customers on an ongoing basis. Without *the bizz,* The Garage could not create a viable business model, be profitable, or secure a sustainable competitive advantage. *The bizz* includes three core components:

- *Leadership and coaching.* Leadership is usually associated with initiative, guiding, and directing. But leadership also includes vision, speaking and listening skills and the ability to provide new ideas. In other words, a leader also has to be a coach. A coach helps you to perform at your greatest capacity; a coach helps you to recognize your own strengths and weaknesses. A coach is different from a boss who tells you what to do. A coach is a mentor, who gives you the tools you need to figure out what to do on your own, who helps you to create new tools.

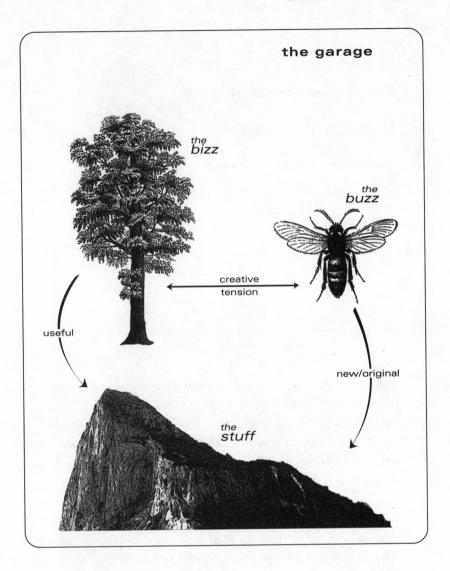

the garage

the *bizz*

the *buzz*

creative tension

useful

new/original

the *stuff*

- *Dynamic business concept (BC) management.* As strategy guru Gary Hamel noted in his book *Leading the Revolution,* "a capacity to first identify, then deconstruct and reconstruct, lies at the heart of a high-performance innovation system. If your company is not experimenting with radically different business models, it's already living on borrowed time."[9] Hamel unpacks a business concept into four major components: core strategy, strategic resources, customer interface,

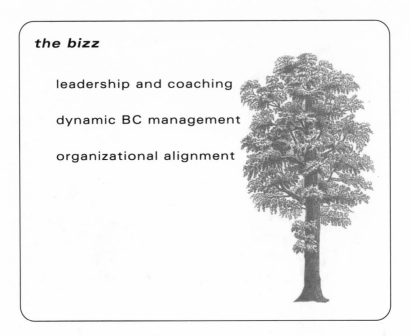

the bizz

> leadership and coaching
>
> dynamic BC management
>
> organizational alignment

and value network. The four components are linked together by three "bridge" components: configuration of activities, customer benefits, and company boundaries. Finally, there are four factors that determine the profit potential of the business model: *efficiency* (the value of customer benefits exceeds the costs of producing them); *uniqueness; fit* (internal consistency among the elements of the business model); and *profit boosters* (such as increasing returns, competitor lockout, economies of scale and scope, and strategic flexibility). Also, it is crucial to view any kind of strategy concepts dynamically. That is, business concept management must be viewed as an ongoing process, not as a static exercise undertaken every three to five years.

- *Organizational alignment.* Sustainable growth and profits, winning loyal customers, and charging them premium prices are not only about business concept formulation; they are also about implementation: making the business concept work. If an organization is properly aligned, it pulls in the right direction—toward growth and profitability. Business strategists have distinguished between *vertical*

the buzz

motivation

communication

interaction

---

alignment, bringing together the strategy of the organization and its people, and *horizontal alignment,* which links the company's actions with customer needs. In both cases, focus and integration are essential. Think of alignment as a set of connected points of focus; without them, an organization wanders and underperforms in implementing its concepts and ideas. As we will show in chapters 4–6, an organization needs to be aligned with respect to technology, its brand promise, and desired customer experience.

the buzz

We will use the term *the buzz* to refer to the process by which The Garage creates a motivating climate of excitement, work satisfaction, and fun. *The buzz* results from a motivating climate within the organization, as well as from appropriate communicative and interactive processes.

Dionysian in spirit, *the buzz* is about Big-Bang creation, passion, and excitement. *The buzz* is the "soft" layer of the organization. The basic orientation of *the buzz* is that of *arousal:* attracting attention; arousing senses, feelings, and intellect; and stirring people to action. Arousal must be managed so that it occurs at the right level: not too much and not too little. If there is too much, it is overwhelming and behavior easily loses focus. If there is too little, the result will be boredom and sluggishness.

Without *the buzz,* work is tedious and the organization cannot perform at its peak. *Buzz* is about shaking things up. *The buzz* consists of the following three interpersonal components:

the buzz and the Bleachmaker

The Clorox Company's Project THINC (Tools and Habits for Inspiring and Nurturing Creativity) is aimed at unleashing creativity in all departments and in each individual employee so that the idea of research and development itself is being reinvented daily. Part of this foray into innovation is "Food for Thought," a program that encourages small groups of about five people to gather over a free lunch and brainstorm for solutions to specific problems. In order to create an innovative culture, Clorox goes beyond the typical gambit of scattering a few posters in the cafeteria to encourage creativity. A big creativity bulletin board in the company's main lobby manifests the centrality of innovative spirit. White boards in the hallways and an online electronic bulletin board allow creativity to permeate the environment, recognizing that the life spring of creative interaction is spontaneous, always flowing, sprouting unexpected tributaries, and revitalizing only insofar as it welcomes contributions from anyone, any time, in any medium.

No floodgates here, and no pretensions. The project also brings in music, toys, games, and goodies because, as we all know from kindergarten (but have sometimes forgotten, perhaps under the influence of the Corporate Undead—see the beginning of this chapter), creativity is stimulated by all our sensory functions and eclecticism, by free interaction and play.

We've always known that Clorox had good *bizz* and *stuff*. Who would have known it had great *buzz* too?

- *Motivation.* Motivation is about both external motivation (i.e., incentives, stock options, fast promotions) and internal motivation (doing interesting work that is in line with personal values). Employees are increasingly interested in connecting workstyles and personal lifestyles. At work, they want to balance corporate demands with personal achievement; in their personal lives, they want to balance personal growth with family life. Today's organizations need to be sensitive to their employees' expectations. To motivate employees effectively, management needs to look at their work and lives holistically. In chapter 3, we offer The Five Individual Workstyle Tools that we have found useful as motivational tools.

- *Communication*. Work-related communications in whatever form must be clear, concise, and relevant. The organization must make sure that communications are pervasive; access to relevant communications must exist everywhere—inside and outside the office on a global scale. To be effective in business now, communications also must be fast. E-mail or telephone turnarounds that take days are unacceptable. In chapter 3, we offer The Five Communication Tools for making communication more effective.

- *Interaction*. Information is shared not only through communication but also through interactions. Interactions range from meetings and joint work-related actions to playing squash. Interactions in The Garage often benefit from being not purely work-related and professional, but engaging and fun, to promote excitement and comradeship. To guarantee the right mix of professionalism and fun, we provide The Five Teamwork Tools in Chapter 3.

the stuff

We use the term *the stuff* to refer to the various resources through which The Garage adds value. *The stuff* is the solid rock of the organization. Without *the stuff,* the organization is—so to speak—just fluff, including lots of talk, hype, and promises that lead nowhere. The tangible output of *the stuff* is the offerings: the goods and services of a business. To create valuable tangible output on an ongoing basis, the organization needs to secure and access certain resources. These resources, which define the essence of *the stuff,* are:

- *Facilities*. Facilities include the offices, the plants, the warehouses of the organization. They need to be top-notch; they need to work; they need to be not too small and not too large. They also need to provide the right working atmosphere, that is, there should be a match between the type of facility and the type of personality working in it, especially as the workplace is changing drastically (see Chapter 4). If there are no facilities in a tangible sense, then the "virtual office" and its interconnectivity is the facility, and the same rules apply.

the stuff

facilities

knowledge and skills

processes

- *Knowledge and skills.* The Garage recruits and trains for certain knowledge and skills. Some of them are communication skills and other "soft skills"; others are management and functional skills. The difficulty, of course, is in getting big companies to unleash innovative drive and capacity in employees who have been schooled in the old control model—and to keep management from quelling it in those who have not yet been tamed. It means that big companies have to break free of their old mind-set. But how do you instill creativity in a culture that deeply fears loss of control? As Murray Low, a professor of entrepreneurship and SCHMITT's colleague at Columbia Business School, puts it: "The challenge is to encourage innovation, creativity, personal passion, and independent initiative in a manner that is consistent with the aims and strategies of the company" and to inspire a "tolerance for honest mistakes."

- *Processes.* Business processes are the operational infrastructure of the organization. We use the term in this book to refer to anything that is complex and includes several steps. Thus, we consider not only supply-chain management to be a process (see Chapter 4) but also branding (see Chapter 5) and service performance as part of customer experience management (see Chapter 6).

We discuss all these resources in more detail in Chapters 4–6, with respect to technology, brands, and customer experience management.

THE CREATIVE TENSION BETWEEN *THE BIZZ* AND *THE BUZZ*

In Chapter 1, we defined *creativity* as something useful and original. Whether we use the term to refer to ideas or actual products, project initiatives or actual innovations, strategic concepts or actual implementations, in a corporate context something creative must always be original and useful for the purpose at hand.

The bizz and *the buzz* of The Garage together will guarantee that something useful and original is created. *The bizz,* the appropriate application of the management rules, assures that something useful is created. *The buzz,* the motivational processes that create excitement, work satisfaction, and fun, assure that something original is created. This useful and original outcome is the ultimate result of a successful resolution of the essential creative tension between *the bizz* and *the buzz.*

Frequently, there is a dichotomy drawn between *the bizz* (the analytical) and *the buzz* (the nonanalytical) side of business. Of course, this dichotomy has long pervaded society and culture as a whole. Throughout modern human history, there have been heated debates between rationalists and romantics, between functionalists and experientialists, between those arguing for order and those arguing for the creative power of chaos.

Business thinkers traditionally have leaned toward the analytical. Business thinkers consider themselves to be rational decision makers. Training in rational, analytical methods and techniques is the key priority in business schools. Business strategists have often argued that companies should be focused on what they do best—usually analytical and operational processes. For example, the idea of core competencies, popularized in the early nineties, is about functional and operational capabilities. In his book *Competitive Advantage,* Michael Porter presents an organization with a choice between "cost leadership and functional product quality." Michael Treacy and Frederik Wiersema, in *The Discipline of Market Leaders,* argue that companies have to focus on one of three value disciplines: operational excellence; product leadership; or customer intimacy (by which they mean superb functional service).

We agree with most business writers that *the bizz* is important. But *the buzz* is equally essential for The Garage. For truly outstanding corporate acts of creativity and innovation, you need both. Most importantly, a tension between the two—if resolved right—creates superior creative output. Both *the bizz* and *the buzz* are thus needed to create great *stuff.*

But how exactly can we make creative use of the tension between *the bizz* and *the buzz* to produce great *stuff?* There are different ways of thinking about this resolution. As we will see, these different ways of thinking will give rise to The Three Tension Resolution Tools as part of The Toolbox of The Garage in Chapter 3.

DIALECTICS

One way to view the creative tension and resolution is in terms of dialectics. According to the philosophy of dialectics, many events in life progress through three stages: *thesis, antithesis,* and *synthesis,* which results from considering the earlier perspectives and arriving at a higher-order truth. Tension resolution is thus about creating higher-order synthesis in business ventures. Of course, over time, the new synthesis will become a new thesis that will stimulate its own antithesis. As a result, the tension between *the bizz* and *the buzz* will always be a dynamic transformational process, propelling the organization to new heights.

An example of creative corporate dialectics is Microsoft's new initiative to transform itself into a company entirely focused on the Internet. The initiative has its roots in Microsoft's earlier thesis to view the world from the perspective of making installations of its Windows software on desktops ubiquitous. Then came the antithesis of embracing the Internet, in terms of its opportunity to sell a new Internet browser (Internet Explorer) and various content Web sites (e.g., sidewalk.com). The lack of lasting success in most of these ventures ultimately led to the synthesis of microsoft.net—described by Bill Gates as "the biggest transition for Mi-

Creativity and Trash Cans

Are you proud of your trash can? What? It never occurred to you? Use your imagination. You could be proud of your trash can if you owned the right one. Visit the Container Store and find out what it feels like. The Container Store is the product of a garage, providing total customer experience by "selling the hard stuff." This, according to company president Kip Tindell, requires courage. And Tindell is right. Just look at the conventions that Tindell breaks by daring to put experience first, not only for the customer but also for the employee.

Transcend value by transcending the rational:

Tindell describes it this way: "Transcending value accrues when you begin to relate emotionally to the product . . . and you live with it every day, and in many cases, for a very long time. It makes an indelible mark on your memory." It's that baseball mitt, he says, that you can slip on to practically relive the catch you made at the end of a glorious season. It's that trash can, "high quality, innovative design, fits in the space in your kitchen perfectly. It looks great and functions beautifully." Don't be afraid: want your customers to love your products. Love them yourself. Translate that love to your employees.

Pay employees what they're really worth:

Tindell urges you to "put your money where your mouth is . . . many retailers are afraid to do that. They must withstand too many pressures from others who don't see the big picture in paying great people well . . . I think it takes more bravery to pay people well than just about anything else." Of course, employee motivation doesn't end with a paycheck. In The Garage, training and meaningful rewards are also key, and the Container Store practices these, prompting *Fortune* magazine to name the Container Store "the best company to work for in America." And the thrill of winning this title increased their *buzz*, creating even greater employee satisfaction and loyalty. Pay employees what they're really worth—not just what the market dictates—and "pay" not just in dollars, but also in training, inspiration, and recognition, and you increase employee worth as they increase the worth of The Garage. It's exponential.

Dare to communicate:

Tindell makes sure that employees are well informed. That they can tell the story of each product as if it were their personal story. So a Nalgene travel bottle becomes worth the dollar or fifty cents more that it costs over the drugstore brand because the customer is just as awed as the salesperson, who relates that the bottle was designed for mountain climbers, and that it will not, at any altitude, under any condition, leak (and ruin that Prada bag you're carrying it in, costing you heartbreak). But here's the risky part: employees are intimately informed not just about products but about the company, its vision, its plans. The Container Store shares just about every kind of information with its employees—even financial information. "Yes, I know that occasionally information falls into the wrong hands," Tindell asserts. "We decided a long time ago, however, that communicating valuable information empowers our employees, strengthens their development, enhances their contributions, and reinforces their loyalty. . . . Being well informed generates that fierce sense of ownership in our company. Customers can feel that energy."

crosoft since the transition from DOS to the Windows operating system."[10] Microsoft.net (abbreviated as .NET) plans to incorporate a new Internet-based operating system into various electronic devices, ranging from smart phones to personal digital assistants to personal computers. The new application will run best on devices that are connected to the Microsoft software code through the .NET infrastructure, thus synthesizing the Internet with the Microsoft operating system. The new initiative also allows Microsoft to rely on an entirely new business model: customers may be billed for their usage of the software rather than for the one-time acquisition of it.

BALANCE

Another way to view the resolution of the tension between *the bizz* and *the buzz* is as the balancing of seeming opposites. This metaphor is based on the yin-yang symbolism that is widespread in East Asian cultures. Yin and yang deals with apparent opposites that, upon closer inspection, turn out to be essential to provide true harmony and balance within the whole. In that vein, tension resolution is about finding the connecting points that create balance in business ventures.

Estée Lauder, one of the world's leading skin care, makeup, fragrance, and hair care makers, sells its brands in more than 100 countries and has applied a balancing approach to the portfolio management of its core brands. The company divides its brand portfolio into two categories: rule-making brands and rule-breaking brands. Rulemakers include the well-established Estée Lauder brands Aramis and Clinique, for example. Rule breakers include several cutting-edge brands that Estée Lauder acquired throughout the 1990s, such as the professional makeup artists' lines Bobby Brown and MAC; Stila; and the pure plant- and flower-based ingredient brand Aveda.

As the polar ends of a spectrum, the rulemakers and rule breakers define each another, not only in company terms but also in the minds of the consumer; they are thus mutually dependent. Rule-breaking brands can learn from the rulemakers how to grow and expand into new target markets, whereas rulemakers can learn innovative marketing ventures from the rule breakers. Most important, as Patrick Bousquet-Chavanne, president of Estée Lauder International, noted, the model allows "collaboration based on shared creativity" across geographic and functional lines.

ALTERNATION

A third way is to consider how *the bizz* and *the buzz* often unfold over time. From a motivational perspective, extended periods of all *bizz* or all *buzz* are counterproductive. Extended periods of *bizz*-like activities result in overstructuring and boredom, which can slow down action. Extended periods of *buzz*-like activities, on the other hand, result in burnout and exhaustion from so much excitement. Thus, there is an ideal balance over time: periods of *bizz* alternating with periods of *buzz*.

Electronic Arts, the world leader of interactive entertainment software, based in Redwood City, California, illustrates this third approach. Like so many fast-growing companies, Electronic Arts has gone through iterations of *bizz* and *buzz*. For example, for years the company focused on growth through acquisitions, acquiring numerous studios worldwide. These acquisitions resulted in a *buzz*—outbursts of innovations in the form of new video games and new features on these games. However, standardization of its look and feel was underutilized, and in 1998–2000 the company turned more attention to its *bizz,* embarking on a major branding initiative to sort out its logo design, brand architecture, and user interface.

SUBOPTIMAL ORGANIZATIONS: DOING WELL IN ONE OR TWO BUT NOT ALL THREE DOMAINS

The Garage manages the creative tension between *bizz* and *buzz* in such a way that it creates great *stuff.* But not all organizations are good at managing this creative tension. Many organizations excel in one domain (e.g., *bizz, buzz,* or *stuff*) or in two but not in all three, and therefore deliver suboptimal performances. Reasons include denial—refusing to acknowledge that these other domains are important—and lack of appropriate management of the other domains. As a result, these suboptimal organizations do not produce ideas, projects, and products that are as creative (useful and original) as they could be. They miss out on one or two critical dimensions.

Suboptimal organizations come in three varieties. First there are unidimensional organizations that are *all stuff, all bizz,* or *all buzz.* Then there are suboptimal organizations that perform well in two but not all three dimensions. Finally, there are organizations known as "sleepers" that have all three components, but none is very strongly developed.

Unidimensional organizations

The *all stuff* organization is obsessed with content. With products, with information, with operations: how great these products are, how incredible people's knowledge and skills are, how wonderfully the machines work.

The *all bizz* organization is full of professional specialists: professional managers, financial planners, accountants, researchers. This organization is obsessed with its concept of professionalism—to its own detriment.

It follows procedures; people follow orders; "smooth operations" is the dictum.

The *all buzz* organization is just about hype and talk and excitement. A powerhouse of brainstorming without a structure that leads anywhere. Uncoordinated activities abound. Dozens and dozens of half-cooked ideas are floating around, none of which are ever reality-tested or taken to the marketplace.

Unidimensional organizations require radical change. They need to give up their exclusive focus and add the key capabilities that they are missing. However, even organizations that do well in two of the three domains are suboptimal. Like the unidimensional organizations, they need to concentrate their hiring, employee training, corporate culture formation, and organizational learning on the missing domain.

Let's take a look at organizations that may have two critical dimensions but still miss out on the third dimension. What are they like?

Two but not three

An organization that has *"stuff + bizz"* has respectable processes and planning procedures and knowledgeable and skillful employees; but it is thrown off when the situation requires individual motivation and initiative, speedy communication, and fast solutions. A good example of this type of organization is the *corporate tower*—the stodgy organization of 10,000+ employees who just come to work to count the hours. Most of the employees in the corporate tower are "technicians." They are quite good at what they do and dutiful in their attendance at endless meetings and long-term planning sessions, but ultimately undermotivated and quite bored. These businesses are well organized and have some quality products, but they can nevertheless lose market share to more innovative competitors. They may also fail to attract the brightest and most creative new employees.

An organization that is *"bizz + buzz"* has all the planning and dynamism it could want, but it is unable to deliver the customer's specific need—whether it is a good, a service, or a simple piece of information. The *B School Start-up* fits this description well—a sort of airy and lofty organization with all the strategies and business models picked up in business school and a group of young and talented company founders that

Urbanfetch: Just *buzz*

Urbanfetch, the online instant delivery retailer, had done a terrific job in New York and London in 2000. In the spring of 2000, SCHMITT ordered a pair of walkie-talkies to speed up communication in SCHMITT's Garage. The walkie-talkie, an awesome palm-sized, Internet Age–looking metallic Motorola, came with a cookie from Urbanfetch. The next day, he ordered another pair—another cookie turned up too. The third day, when SCHMITT ordered three pairs of walkie-talkies (all matching the color of his new Razor Scooter), Urbanfetch gave him a really cool T-shirt. By the end of the week, a service representative from Urbanfetch was on the phone thanking him for his daily walkie-talkie shopping spree. The following Monday, an e-mail labeled "You've been bad . . ." arrived from Urbanfetch. It said:

> I will not go to the same deli and order the same sandwich again.
> I will not go to the same deli and order the same sandwich again.
> I will not go to the same deli and order the same sandwich again.
> I will not go to the same deli and order the same sandwich again.
> I will not go to the same deli and order the same sandwich again.
> I will not go to the same deli and order the same sandwich again.
> I will not go to the same deli and order the same sandwich again.
> I will not go to the same deli and order the same sandwich again.
> I will not go to the same deli and order the same sandwich again.
> I will not go to the same deli and order the same sandwich again.
> I will not go to the same deli and order the same sandwich again.

> Xando Cosi—New York's #1 Sandwiches and Salads. Now Delivered Fresh From Urbanfetch. 24/7. And for a limited time, buy 3 and the fourth sandwich is free. Lunch will never be the same . . . What can we fetch for you?

Now, that's awesome *buzz!*

Unfortunately, all its *buzz* could not save its consumer business from dot-com extinction, because the company was *buzz* only and lacked a rigorous business model. Although Urbanfetch had secured $70 million in private financing, the costs proved too high for the company to survive, just like its competitor, *Kozmo.com.*

lack sufficient knowledge and skills of the real marketplace. It produces a brilliant and original business plan, but is unable to execute it, or to establish a consumer base. It is also this kind of organization, for example, that produces and markets cool-looking products that simply do not work well.

An organization that is *"stuff + buzz"* may have great resources, knowledgeable and skilled engineers, and motivated and creative employees, but it lacks simple planning processes and organizational alignment. It has a buzzing environment and interesting products or technologies, but little experience with strategy and planning, and with logistics. Everybody knows the *brilliant failed business,* perhaps the most tragic variety of suboptimal organizations. Everything is improvised. Communications work well because people like each other, but everything is done ad hoc. Corporate artists abound in this environment. They know one domain and they know how to motivate others with their excitement, but they lack professional management skills. As a result, they are ideal prey for takeovers.

The sleeper

Finally, there is one more type of suboptimal organization: the sleeper. The sleeper has all three components, but in a rudimentary state of development. Some of these sleepers have been in hibernation for years. The technique for waking them up, however, is different from the learning and development needed for the other suboptimal organizations. Sleepers need a harsh wake-up call and someone who provides creativity leadership across *the stuff, the bizz,* and *the buzz.* Many monopolies fall into this category, and deregulation sometimes provides the wake-up call.

SUMMARY

In this chapter, we have presented a model of corporate creativity that we will use throughout the book. This model—based on the idea of The Garage—brings together the analytical and rational planning side of business, *the bizz,* with the passionate and dynamic side of business, *the buzz,* to produce creative *stuff.* In The Garage, there is a tension between *the bizz* and *the buzz,* a tension that captures and nurtures chaos. The result of managing this tension is creative outcomes.

Many organizations are suboptimal, that is, they fall short of being a garage because they are missing one or two of the above three components or because these components are underdeveloped. Thus, the key goal for most organizations is to unleash its hidden creativity. In the next chapter, we present The Blueprint and The Toolbox of The Garage—a set of principles, approaches, and techniques that can be used to generate and improve corporate creativity and sustain it over time. The Blueprint and Toolbox are excellent practical starting points for transforming an organization into a garage.

the blueprint and the toolbox of the garage

Now that we have a clear understanding of what The Garage is, we can look more closely at what goes on inside—at the general skills, processes, and techniques that are used to manage chaos and to free up creativity and innovation. We also present proven tools to promote individual and collaborative creativity, in specific projects. In this chapter, we present management concepts that are useful for organizing the entire company and for unleashing creativity in all sorts of corporate projects.

To get us started, the following business parable, set at a corporate retreat, shows the unexpected way that creativity can work for an individual in a team setting.

"I Lost My Business Plan in the Woods"

At first Carol had dreaded it. She was head of Customer Insight—what was she doing at a corporate strategy retreat? Waste of time. Corporate mumbo jumbo was corporate mumbo jumbo, whether you were in a

She had left
the conference center just as

the pale sunlight was showing on the tops of the trees.
The stone gazebo at the overlook point was still in shade.

concrete canyon or off at a retreat in the woods. Twenty-two executives from a business hotel chain communing with nature. But the CEO had insisted she attend. So she had taken it as an opportunity for personal growth: every morning she got up early to go running through the woods that engulfed the conference center.

The running alleviated the routine quality of the retreat's meetings, like the one she sat in now. Expansion. Tom Kelley was making a presentation, his Brooks Brothers sleeves rolled up, PowerPoint slides blazing away.

Carol's mind drifted off. She remembered the run she had taken earlier in the day. She had left the conference center just as the pale sunlight was showing on the tops of the trees. The stone gazebo at the overlook point was still in shade.

She loved being alone, hearing nothing but her own footsteps and her own breathing, enjoying the chill of the air and the smell of the woods. Her new running shoes hugged her feet and cushioned her footfalls. Nike: $139. The very latest high-tech model—VisiZoom Air—even Kelley had remarked how cool they were. Does it matter? she wondered, feeling the bark on the path shift under her feet. Is that why I run?

She sucked in the scent of the pines. The smell reminded her of Christmas trees . . . from her childhood. Real trees. Shaking the snow off them before they came into the house, waiting for the branches to dry before putting on the strings of lights. Sneaking downstairs late at night to plug in the lights and sit in the silent room in the soft warm glow. The overall light was always pink—all the colored lights combined to make pink. Why was that? Every ornament was different in those days: little musical instruments and toys, snow scenes, Santa Claus. Everything with its own identity and personality.

In her mind, Carol ran again past a driveway and caught a glimpse of some tennis courts. Suddenly she stopped and turned back. She walked up the little drive closer to the courts. A fine coating of fresh new morning dew rested lightly on the grounds and the benches and the surrounding greenery. The scene reminded her of the movie *Blow-Up*. A tennis match with no ball.

"But this strategy is not compatible with our mission," Tom said.

"Whatever our mission is."

The scene reminded her of the movie *Blow-Up*.
A tennis match with no ball. "But this strategy is

not compatible with our mission," Tom said.

"No, I disagree. We stand for quality, and customer relations. No other business hotel chain can beat us in that. That's what it says and that's what it means to me, and I can damn well assure you that . . ."

That sort of business babble always anesthetized Carol. She drifted off again.

Walking now, up a gentle hill. A metal gate blocked the path, designed to keep cars out of the woods: Carol slipped around it. The trees became thicker, the air cooler and more fragrant. Suddenly there in the woods to her right, at the crest of the hill. Was it a fallen tree? A meteor from outer space?

She climbed the little hill and approached the thing. A statue. A stone statue placed in the middle of the woods. A small placard at its base identified it: *Reclining Nude.*

She touched it, felt the coolness, caressed it, and then looked guiltily around. How afraid we are of touch, of sense. Suddenly she noticed the quiet. And then the sounds within it. Birds. Noisy as hell, really—jays. Why had she never heard them?

Listening, she jogged on down the path. Another, smaller statue appeared. Thicker, lower to the ground, undulating. *Seated Nude,* said the placard. A sculpture garden, *au naturel,* she thought, congratulating herself on the pun. Again she reached out. Her hand stroked the Nude's cool, slightly wet skin.

It reminded her of Lawrence. Lawrence had been the VP of Marketing—she ran into him once in a while but hadn't really known him. One evening, at a company party, they had gotten drunk. Who else was there? Late in the evening, Lawrence had stood and posed as a sculpture, motionless in the ballroom. Everyone fell silent. Or maybe she was the only one there. She couldn't remember. Clear green eyes and smooth brown skin. It was mesmerizing. And then the cold feeling of the podium pressed against her sweating back, the same podium where the CEO had delivered his speech a few hours earlier. For the next two weeks, Carol had passed by his office nearly every day. Then Lawrence left. No one ever saw him after that. He just checked out. How did that happen to people?

Suddenly there was a noise behind her, and she turned around. A bear. Damn—a bear! Its tiny eyes fixed on her. She almost screamed.

A metal gate blocked the path,
designed to keep cars out of the woods:

Carol slipped around it.

Her hand stroked the cool, slightly wet skin.
It reminded her of

Lawrence ... the VP of marketing.

She was running again, before she knew what she was doing. *Shouldn't run—don't provoke it. Defending its territory. Instinct, peabrain, synapses. Too late.* She ran. The bear followed, its breath coming short and sharp. Red mouth rimmed by black fur. Carol ran up the path where she had jogged yesterday, up to a small clearing where a herd of satellite dishes stood corralled by a chain-link fence. What were they doing in the woods? The bear wouldn't follow her here. Electromagnetic field. Too exposed. Safety.

When she looked around again, the bear was not there.

She clung to the chain-link fence, panting, her sweat cooling on her face. The satellite dishes hummed. Were they moving? Trying to get out. *The Day of the Triffids.* The humming became louder, harsher. Something was wrong.

"Carol, what's your perspective on this? Do you think we should expand in this region? What about downtown Detroit? How would you evaluate the potential?"

Startled, Carol managed to reply, "I'm not wild about Detroit."

"That's what I figured," came the reply.

The talk went on among them. Carol breathed a sigh of relief.

Reversing her course, she began jogging again back down the hill she'd come up. Then faster, her stride lengthening as she ran downhill. Always turning left, she realized, imperceptibly to the left. When she passed the *Reclining Nude* again, she realized that she was running in an almost complete circle. It had not occurred to her before. The power station was really just a few steps from the *Reclining Nude.* Just a big circle. Why hadn't she seen this?

She sat down. Dreamed. *What if I remain here forever? Not go to the meeting, just stay here. They'd look for me for a while. Then they'd forget. I'd eat grass. Live like the bear. Forgotten. Or the lake. Heavy stone self, sinking, resting on the bottom forever. "Unbewusst, höchste Lust." Forget . . .*

"*Carol, where is the business plan?*" They must have been yelling at her for a while.

She stared at them with alarm. Her dream had vanished. What was left?

"Earth to Carol . . . Where's the business plan?"

Taking a deep breath, she said, "I lost my business plan in the woods."

They were all silent for a moment. Carol had always been a little

Carol ran up the path ... where a herd of satellite
dishes stood corralled by a chain link fence.

What were they doing in the woods?

weird, but this was extreme even for her. They looked at Tom. He could usually translate.

Tom stared at Carol. And then he laughed. "The woods? Expand into the woods?"

Another moment passed, then they all jumped in.

"Yeah, like this facility. A retreat in the woods!"

"No, a hotel in the woods. A business hotel in the woods! Fully functional, but in a setting like this."

"But not far from major urban centers. We could find locations like this."

"It's a new vision for the company—no one else is doing this; no one else has even thought of this. It's great!"

"Awesome. Carol, this is awesome."

"Incredible customer insight! She blows my mind."

WHAT DOES THE BUSINESS PARABLE MEAN?

And the moral of the story is . . . feel free to space out in meetings? Well, not exactly. To find the moral, we have to dig a bit deeper.

First, note why Carol is at the meeting in the first place. What did the CEO have in mind, sending a Customer Insight specialist to a strategy retreat? We can only speculate. Perhaps it was part of his or her blueprint to foster creativity by bringing together seemingly incongruent corporate worlds.

Now let's look at Carol. As she daydreams through the meeting, she recalls vividly the experiences she has had earlier in the day. Carol is exceptionally sensitive to her environment: she allows things to affect her, to challenge her, to make her wonder. Her mind is freely associative. She pursues thoughts that others might dismiss and seems unconstrained by assumptions. And because of these characteristics, she imagines other realities. Her generative imagination may not produce the answer to the question that's being asked, but she may just end up answering a more important question instead.

Here's where her colleagues come in. They recognize Carol as "a little weird." But they listen, and try to make sense of what she's said—Tom is the "translator." And here is a crucial tool of creativity: rather than reject something because it seems odd or because you don't understand it, try instead to see what you can make of it. Carol's colleagues look for meaning in her obscure comment, and it leads them to generate the new and exciting business idea. What does Carol mean when she says, "I left my business plan in the woods"? Who knows? But her colleagues give it a vibrant and relevant meaning for their company.

THE BLUEPRINT AND TOOLS

In this chapter we present The Blueprint and The Toolbox of The Garage. The Blueprint of The Garage are detailed and coordinated programs of action for harnessing corporate creativity. This blueprint includes, first, a clear statement of the importance of creativity in the corporation at large and in work projects as well as guidelines on how a company intends to use creative (i.e., useful and new) initiatives and secure competitive advantage through creativity. Another part of The Blueprint includes the issue of how to set up a garage structurally. Finally, there is the issue of recruiting and rewarding creative talent. The Blueprint of The Garage is a broad-based structural and process-guided initiative. As such, the work on The Blueprint must be initiated by senior management.

The Toolbox of The Garage, on the other hand, contains specific devices for using and leveraging creativity at daily work as individuals or teams in a corporate setting. They include three types of tools: Working Tools for individual creativity and teamwork; Communication Tools; and, most important, Resource Tools for managing the creative tension between *bizz* and *buzz* as well as for exploring new issues in original ways.

The Blueprint and The Toolbox need to be applied hand-in-hand. It is The Blueprint and The Toolbox of The Garage that guarantee the right relation between *bizz, buzz,* and *stuff,* thus transforming chaos into creative initiatives, in the form of either corporation-wide or project-specific undertakings.

MAKING CREATIVITY A PRIORITY

In The Garage, developing, capturing, and disseminating creative ideas are the top business priority. Many organizations, as we saw in the previous chapter, fall short of this goal. Many organizations do not even under-

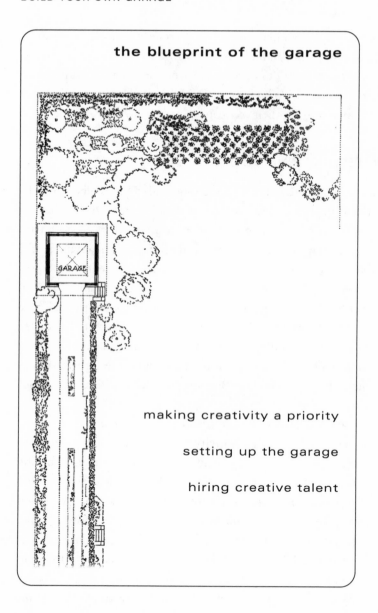

the blueprint of the garage

GARAGE

making creativity a priority

setting up the garage

hiring creative talent

stand what creativity means. They consider creativity to be of minor importance from a management perspective and something that is specific only to certain departments (such as marketing, R&D, and design departments). They do not see creativity as something with which senior management should concern itself. The "creatives" are often regarded as

Creativity Misunderstood

Creativity is often envisioned as the unplanned outburst of energy that, in a wink, is supposed to result in cutting-edge projects and products that will change the face of the organization overnight. Many corporate creativity initiatives focus on this aspect of creativity—from techniques like "Creativity Kick Starts," "Idea Recording," "Mind-Mapping," "Visual Thinking Techniques," and "Mental Workout Center" to activities in which employees are supposed to free their unconscious from the constraints of daily corporate life through all sorts of playful group activities, like jumping on a trampoline or heading into the woods.

However, for many years, psychologists have stressed that creativity is not only a "freewheeling," "brainstorming," "going-off-in-all-different-directions" phenomenon. Equally important is the "attention-guided," "brain-focusing," "bringing-it-all-together" element of creativity. Without this more structured phase, creative ideas are just original, but not really useful. As part of the creative process, we need both "divergent" and "convergent" thinking, and in an organization we need both "divergent" and "convergent" thinkers. An organization that makes creativity a priority needs to embrace this complex nature of creativity and communicate such complexity at all levels.[11]

slightly offbeat, mad geniuses—necessary but weird—definitely not front-office material. While mainstream corporate culture may admire their work, it has little idea what they actually do, how they do it, and what relevance creativity itself may have for the business as a whole.

SETTING UP A GARAGE

There are several ways of setting up a garage. Each one has its own opportunities and challenges.

First, you can buy a garagelike company. Acquisitions can be expensive, and—as we have seen in this chapter's business parable—the challenge of an acquisition strategy is to keep the garagelike spirit of the acquired company alive, as the vampire story illustrated.

One alternative to acquisition is to incubate a garage internally or externally with the objective of ultimately incorporating it into the organization. Siemens has done it. McKinsey has done it. Ernst & Young has done it. Numerous other companies have started their incubators or "accelerators," providing start-ups with financial resources and management expertise.

The idea is to circumvent the slow and bureaucratic internal new product development process and to develop ideas that are faster and more radical and that have the potential of generating large returns for the company. Incubators, however, can pose cultural challenges and often do not deliver on the garagelike mentality that is expected from them. To be true incubators, the new ventures must be independent; members should receive stock options, and they should be able to compete freely for support—this is rarely the case.

The best way, and the hardest but also most rewarding way in the long term, is to create your own garage internally. Unlike the two prior approaches, creating an internal garage requires a serious commitment to corporate transformation. Structurally, the transformation process may be tested by first setting up a smaller quasi-independent structure, then letting it pervade the entire organization and gradually transform it. Moreover, setting up a garage internally is often less expensive than buying it and less risky than incubating it because established and known resources can be used as part of the development. Challenges include who to select to be part of the team and how to let that team run as wild as necessary, at least in the early stages of the initiative. Established cultural constraints may restrain the effort to such an extent that it may hardly deserve the term *garage*.

Ford's eConsumer Group is an example of setting up a garage within a large organization. After learning some agonizing lessons in the 1980s, U.S. car manufacturer Ford was determined not to be left behind again, no matter how frightening it may be to keep up.[12] To that end, Ford has set up an eConsumer Group to explore and implement the myriad possibilities that the Internet offers the auto industry—including building-to-order, partnerships with other online businesses, supply-chain management, tracking factory-to-dealer channels, and even Internet-enabled cars. But the specific products and services that Ford's team is able to develop are arguably less important than the effect it is having on the way business gets done at Ford. The transformation has been a gradual one, but the eConsumer Group is showing its old school colleagues how things get done in a fast business environment.

It all began with making a quiet end run around senior management. Jim Schroer, one of the Group's executive sponsors, explains: "While senior executives here were having difficulty hitting the 'reply' button on their e-mail, Thor built this whole team." Thor Ibsen is the company's Internet leader. "[The team members] didn't know what couldn't be done, and they were too naive to know what needed approval. The secret was let 'em run, and make sure that none of the organization's white blood cells got in the way."

From the beginning, it was clear that the eConsumer Group would not be conducting business as usual. In order to make an impact at Ford, the Group has had to do things in new and flexible ways. It started with hiring—the Group looked for people who were comfortable with change and with a certain lack of structure; questions from interviewees like "What is my job description?" or "Can I see an org chart?" were taken as signals that the candidate might not have the right mind-set. Budgeting is another area that remaims flexible; although he does not have access to infinite resources, Ibsen has arranged a rolling budget that allows him to allocate funds on an as-needed basis. Within the Group, hierarchy is unimportant. In the words of Jeff Liedel, the team's director of technology, "Everyone reports to everyone else." And Ibsen uses this openness to strategic advantage in his dealings with the rest of the company. For instance, it is not unusual for a member of the group to present a new idea to executives four steps up the hierarchy; in this way, status and its ensuing struggles for power are rendered irrelevant.

The Group's members enjoy a degree of autonomy and responsibility normally not seen in a corporation of Ford's size and stature. According to Ibsen, "The only way we can keep so many balls in the air is to have a lot of jugglers and to trust them—not always checking to see whether they're juggling it the right way. Once we establish a common vision and a shared purpose, I don't want to know what my team members are doing day to day. I trust them."

HIRING FOR CREATIVITY

Identify whether an employee is qualified to be part of an organization, whether they perform their jobs well, and whether they need additional training. When organizations recruit and hire managers and other employees, they look for certain backgrounds, experiences, and skills. In their day-to-day management, these managers and employees use a variety of planning, assessment, and measurement instruments. As part of learning and education programs, managers and employees attend executive training. All these tools and techniques roughly fall into the three categories of *the bizz, the buzz,* and *the stuff.*

To assess *stuff* qualifications in a hiring situation, the recruiter may present an intelligence test or look for knowledge in certain areas (mathematics, engineering, history, and so on). *Bizz* qualifications are assessed during an interview via certain psychological tests or scenarios. Finally, for *the buzz,* there are tests for lateral and divergent thinking for recruitment situations, as well as various background checks (in terms of unusual hobbies, interests, and activities).

THE TOOLBOX OF THE GARAGE

The Toolbox of The Garage contains a set of specific tools that harness corporate creativity. Let's open up The Toolbox of The Garage and take a look at its three drawers. One drawer contains the *working tools* of The Garage. A second contains the *communication tools;* and the third drawer contains the *resource tools.*

THE WORKING TOOLS

The working tools enable The Garage to engage in acts of individual creativity and to produce creativity and innovation through teamwork. The Five Individual Workstyle Tools below define how an individual person generally relates to his or her own work. As we will illustrate, each one has a *bizz* and a *buzz* aspect to it. In contrast, The Five Teamwork Tools define how individuals in a team should relate to other team members to achieve a common goal. Again, each one has a *bizz* and a *buzz* component to it.

Spotting Qualifications for Creativity

Psychologists have been banging their heads against their one-way mirrors, spying on their subjects for decades trying to schematize a set of characteristics that can consistently identify the "creative" individual. The problem? Creative individuals are the hardest people to pigeonhole. Nevertheless, these studies have given us some crude guidelines that fall into two areas: problem-solving style and personality. Here are the charts: An employee with a creative problem-solving style

- would sooner innovate than improve
- has fresh perspectives on old problems
- copes with several new ideas at the same time
- is not methodical or systematic
- does not impose strict order on matters within his/her own control
- seeks to bend or break the rules
- often risks doing things differently
- can stand out in disagreement against the group
- acts without proper authority

So far, so good. Those criteria could identify the digital whiz kid who just shot a digital video. Or they could just as easily fit the campus crank who plasters your lobby walls with flyers when he's not busy befriending pigeons. Let's see if the second set of guidelines gives us further help.

An employee with a generally creative personality is

- Clever
- Humorous
- Informal
- Insightful
- Inventive
- Original
- Reflective
- Resourceful
- Self-confident
- Sexy
- Snobbish
- Unconventional

Okay. But a lot of these qualities won't necessarily come out during an interview. And the few that do come out (sexy, self-confident, clever) may trick you into false hopes that could be disappointed. These lists are not a waste of space; they're helpful to a degree, but they try to define qualities that can't be put in a box. How do you recognize a creative type? We would venture to say it takes one to know one. Keep that in mind when you're deciding who will do the hiring.

Once they are hired, here are some additional suggestions: accept that some people are probably more inherently creative than others; accept that some people have hidden creativity that can be released and tapped. And every time you see the word *accept,* challenge it in your mind and in your practices. Unleashing creativity in creative people might depend on transforming the company culture so that everyone feels they have the potential to be creative. Who cares whether creative people are born or made? Operate without assumptions about this and maximize the factors that can enhance creativity. Shake down the hierarchies. Increase the flow of communication and trust (see the box on the Container Store in chapter 2).

Keep your feet off the brake pedal when an employee's imagination takes a sudden curve. Reward communication; reward creativity even when it is not immediately implemented. Don't dismiss ideas that are simply ahead of their time—modes of implementation must respond to creativity, not vice versa. And above all, reduce the level of stress that comes from making employees feel that they must always have "the right solution." There is a tendency to reinforce the idea that the right solution is tried and true. Just as often, the best solutions are ones that have never been tried before. They are innovations that will advance the way we think and do business.

The Five Individual Workstyle Tools are

- *Tool 1: Think big and pay attention to the small details.* "I like thinking big. I always have. To me, it's very simple: if you're going to be thinking anyway, you might as well think big," writes architect Rem Koolhaas in a book appropriately titled *S, M, L, XL.*[13]

    However, in each stage of execution, it is key to pay attention to the little details. Some of the best big thoughts have failed because

the
working
tools

the
communication
tools

the
resource
tools

the toolbox of the garage

they were not executed with the necessary attention to detail. So, how do you get a person to think big and pay attention to the details? Getting somebody to think big is a matter of motivation and providing challenging targets; that is, it is a *buzz* process. Paying attention to details is a matter of detailed control; that is, it is a *bizz* process. Big thinkers may resist control. If you are a big thinker, you must find motivation as well by seeing the value of *the bizz*. Don't stand in its way.

- *Tool 2: Be reflective in planning and determined in execution.* Planning requires the skills of analysis and structuring. It requires background research (on a broad scale). Execution requires networking and swift action. The two need to go hand-in-hand. Once you have made up your mind, execute with full power and determination, focusing on one goal. Combine *the bizz* in planning with *the buzz* in execution.

- *Tool 3: Don't duplicate; innovate.* In your work, it is important to be open to the ideas and work of others (e.g., your competitors). Benchmarking is key for day-to-day *bizz* competitive assessment and extremely important for new idea generation: for identifying how something can be done; for identifying strengths and shortcomings in thought and execution. However, you should never strive for duplication. When you encounter a successful example, think first about how to mimic it but then how to surpass it. When you encounter an unsuccessful example, ask yourself what made it fail and make sure you circumvent or overcome these obstacles. In other words, create a *buzz* to top the successful and to get the unsuccessful to work.

- *Tool 4: Be accountable for mistakes, but unafraid of risks.* You should be accountable; be responsible when something goes wrong; analyze what went wrong and avoid excuses. It is part of good *bizz* to be accountable. However, you should not take it too far. Don't let blaming yourself prevent you from moving forward or taking new risks. Use the analysis to motivate yourself, to move forward, to create new *buzz*.

- *Tool 5: Always keep a creative tension.* Hold the creative tension between *the bizz* and *the buzz*. This tension is the starting point of creating something big. It is the starting point of creativity. You may feel overwhelmed by the uncertainty, by the chaos. But as Nietzsche said, "One must nurture chaos in oneself to give birth to a dancing star."

In today's work environment, most of us do not work alone but as part of a team. The Five Individual Workstyle Tools that we just discussed are used primarily for individual work, although they may also be useful as principles for teamwork. The Five Teamwork Tools that follow are exclusively for collaborative work.

The Five Teamwork Tools are

- *Tool 1: Know your strengths and those of others, and then trust them.* It is important to know your strengths and the strengths of others. Once you do, you can delegate; let others do certain work, and, most important, you can then trust them to get things done in a competent way. That is good *bizz.* By working this way, you also create positive *buzz.* It is a mistake to strive to be the center of attention all the time or to sit too long on the sidelines. Everyone needs to contribute what he or she can, and trust creates an open path for motivating contributions.

- *Tool 2: Enjoy the interaction in the group, and be critical but constructive.* In a real team, team members derive a lot of satisfaction from their joint work. But not all ideas are of equal quality, because of variations in individual strengths. Low-quality ideas need to be identified and edited. Uncensored brainstorming is a waste of time; it's bad *bizz* and can lead to frustration. The group should enjoy the results of the interaction. There is a lot of fun in creating something big together, and in recognizing quality ideas. That's *the buzz.*

- *Tool 3: Have a creative thinker, an implementer, and a buffer in the team.* Different people in a team will have different skills. In fact, a team that is homogenous in terms of skills (e.g., only hyper-fueled big thinkers, or only plan-oriented implementers) will not work. Therefore, group composition is important. You need a creative thinker for the ideas, an implementer to keep work focused and get things done, and a buffer for smoothing out interactions and communications.

- *Tool 4: Utilize quiet times to prepare for intense periods.* In any extended project, there will be times when not much seems to happen. That's the nature of creativity. Psychologists have called it "the incubation period." Then suddenly there is a burst and a rush of activity toward completion. Enjoy work in both periods. Utilize the calm before the storm. Enjoy the alternation of *bizz* and *buzz*.

- *Tool 5: Celebrate completions, but never be satisfied.* To be proud of an achievement as a team and to celebrate it is a key positive feedback mechanism. You need it; it's good for *the buzz*. But don't rest on your laurels. In fact, the time immediately after completing a project presents a good opportunity to identify weaknesses (that's *bizz*). These insights can then be used as input for the next project that gets *the buzz* going again. After a brief quiet period (see Tool 4), start thinking about how to surpass what you have just created.

THE COMMUNICATION TOOLS

Communication flows smoothly within The Garage. In addition, The Five Communication Tools ensure that communication is prompt, appropriate, and goal-directed.

The Five Communication Tools are

- *Tool 1: Communicate with clarity.* Give clear instructions. Present clearly. Don't be afraid of directness. Don't be vague. Use examples for abstract concepts.

- *Tool 2: Communicate concisely.* Don't write excessively long reports or e-mails. Follow a logical structure: in paragraph one, say why you're writing. In a presentation, present your recommendation first, then give the background. Be brief. Don't clutter your presentation slides. Always communicate the few essential things forcefully rather than too many things.

- *Tool 3: Provide time frames.* For any action item, give a time frame when you want it completed. Insist on the completion date, and check at reasonable intervals to make sure the date is still realistic. If it is not, stick to it as a goal but mentally calculate the added couple of hours or days that may be needed. Be concerned if it is not done after the (mentally granted) extension period. Be sure to communicate appropriately if others will need notification.

- *Tool 4: Share information.* In today's business world where networking, digitization, and speed count, sharing of information enhances productivity immensely. Moreover, The Garage needs to have the technology for sharing information and using it to involve relevant others. Networks must be clearly defined and instantly accessible.

- *Tool 5: Use an action frame to communicate.* Insist on being told precisely what you are expected to do. Give others instructions about what you want them to do. Present the analysis as an attachment. Always be action-oriented.

THE RESOURCE TOOLS

Our third drawer contains the Resource Tools of The Garage. The Resource Tools are higher-order management tools.

There are two kinds of Resource Tools. Creative Tension Resolution Tools allow a garage to make the most of the tension between its *bizz* and its *buzz.* Creative Exploration Tools are tools that help The Garage to examine and analyze its initiatives in creative and original ways.

Creative Tension Resolution Tools

In chapter 2, we discussed the fact that *the bizz* and *the buzz* are often in conflict. In fact, we argued that the resolution of the tension between these two elements produces the very essence of creativity. Unfortunately, most of the so-called creativity techniques that are commercially available never address this creative tension, nor do they offer procedures for its resolution. The framework of The Garage is based on the idea that *the bizz* and *the buzz,* while often in conflict and tension, are not mutually exclusive.

The goal therefore is to use this tension—and that is what the *Creative*

Communication Rules in The Garage

Three simple rules define communications in The Garage. First, *use your communication tools to maximize networking, digitization, and speed.* You know how to use all of them, and you know each device's strengths and limitations. That means that in The Garage, you have a clear priority for e-mail. You use the phone if you can communicate faster or reach a decision faster by phone than by e-mail, or when you need to speak on a personal basis. You avoid fax. It's a pest. It is an old-fashioned technology used excessively by inferior companies. (In fact, you can judge how inefficient a company is by the ratio of fax to e-mail usage.) Faxing wastes people's time; you can just as well send an e-mail (with a scanned-in attachment). Finally, reserve face-to-face meetings for special occasions. Never meet "just to touch base" or "to see how we could collaborate" unless there is a specific proposal. If somebody asks for a one-hour meeting, suggest a ten-minute phone call as an alternative—trust us, they won't need more. If they say they want just five minutes of your time, expect to talk for fifteen minutes. Minimize unnecessary encounters if you can.

Second, *check your e-mail, phone, and fax messages frequently, at the very least once a day.* In responding to communications, you do not believe in excessive prioritizing. You never look at an e-mail and say, "I'll answer it later." You look at something, or listen to it, and you respond promptly. You don't accumulate unanswered messages because you know this leads to procrastination. As a matter of good *bizz,* you should check e-mails and voice mails wherever you are—worldwide. There is absolutely no excuse for anybody (no matter what rank) not to get back to someone within a couple of days. There is also no excuse for not answering an e-mail, at least very briefly, even if you are not interested in the communication.

Third, *always have the latest devices and know how to use them (at least the basics).* You know how to attach video and audio files to e-mails; how to open and save all sorts of attachments; and how to reply and forward. You have a mobile phone, and have invested at least a few hundred dollars in a quality fax machine to avoid paper jams. (Of course, you use the fax machine primarily for receiving messages from the Corporate Undead, not sending them.) You believe in quality communications devices. If your company does not pay for the best, buy your own; these devices are inexpensive and they save you time and headaches. Also, be sure you have your own devices; when you share, you will almost certainly miss critical information.

Tension Resolution Tools are for. Whenever you are challenged for a creative solution—as an individual, as a team, or as an organization—you may use any of the following three tools. Note that they may be used verbally or visually, for a tangible outcome or a more abstract situation. They are truly creative process management tools that capitalize on the tension between *the bizz* and *the buzz*.

- *Tool 1:* The first tool—*creative synthesis*—results from the dialectical method. Try to formulate the Apollonian as the thesis and the Dionysian as the antithesis and create a synthesis of *the bizz* and *the buzz*. For example, in a new product design for a portable computer, the Apollonian perspective may argue for functionality, simple standardized features, and ease of use. The *buzz* perspective may be to add a few extra bells-and-whistles to the design to make the computer seem "alive." The synthesis will consist of functional features that communicate the "organic aspect of the computer," such as the pulsating light that Apple has designed for its iMac to indicate that the computer is asleep.

- *Tool 2:* The second tool—*creative balancing*—results from the yinyang view. Creative balancing is useful for balancing *the bizz* and *the buzz* and seeing them as actually mutually dependent. For example, think about how to put together a creative team. You can't just have the freewheeling, associative, and "big picture" thinkers in that team. You also need people who get things done and are well versed in project management; in fact, one will need the other to drive the project forward. And, significantly, your team will operate more creatively if it includes members strongly focused in each of these areas—rather than a group where everyone has equally moderate *bizz* and *buzz* talents.

- *Tool 3:* The third tool—*creative oscillation*—is a process for managing *the bizz* and *the buzz* over time. One application is the type of core processes an organization needs to focus on at various periods or seasons. Imagine you are a toy manufacturer. During the prime time before and after Christmas sales, you should concentrate all resources on the *bizz* process of distribution, logistics planning, in-

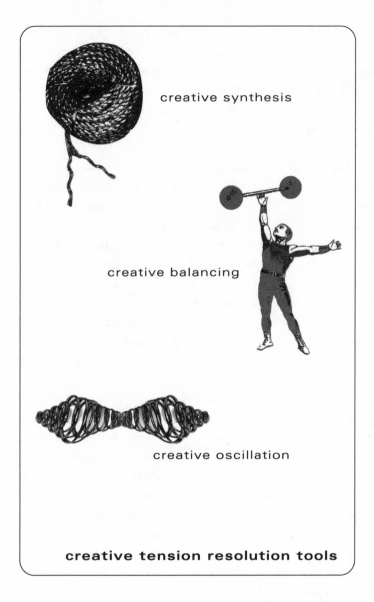

creative synthesis

creative balancing

creative oscillation

creative tension resolution tools

voicing, and so on. The post-Christmas lull may be a good brief quiet time to utilize, and early spring may be a good time for *buzz* processes such as trying out new approaches and doing so in an interactive setting. You may then intersperse a planning period in the early summer and oscillate a few times before the fall frenzy starts.

stripping
and
dressing

focusing
and
broadening

exploring
in a
new context

creative exploration tools

Creative Exploration Tools

The last set of resource tools is the *creative exploration tools*. These are tools for viewing and analyzing issues in creative and original ways. They can be used to examine any issue essential to the organization: a brand, an initiative, an event, or a process.

The first creative exploration tool—*"stripping and dressing"*—is useful for getting at the essence of something and for differentiating the essence from the nonessential. Note that the nonessential may also fulfill important functions, but those are in a way additional decorative functions that are optional, though they are not essential. For example, imagine for a moment the interior—or the so-called trade dress—of a Starbucks shop. In terms of the visual, auditory, textile, and other sensory elements in this retail space, there are numerous things to notice. The coffee cups and the wallpaper; the sound of the espresso machine; the conversations between customers and service people; the serving station; the seats and couches; and so on. Now imagine you are interested in determining the core of the Starbucks brand in a sensory sense. Using the "stripping and dressing" tool, you could start by listing all the many sensory elements and then strip Starbucks' trade dress down. Eliminate the nonessentials. As you are gradually stripping the brand, you may discuss with others—at each exploration point—whether you need to probe further, and why. You will ultimately arrive at the essence of the brand. That is, if you took off any of these core elements, the brand would be empty—no longer Starbucks. You have now arrived at the core of the Starbucks brand in a sensory sense. These are the sensory elements essential to the experience of Starbucks.

Next, you may want to use the reverse procedure, dressing up the brand again, perhaps with a certain strategic objective in mind (e.g., Starbucks wants to increase its market penetration among the teen segment; or Starbucks wants to have a broader presence in people's homes rather than in stores; or Starbucks will expand into a certain geographic region). Again, you record your reasons at each exploration step—now in terms of why additional dress might be needed. Stripping and dressing is a fun exercise. SCHMITT once performed it with a fashion client by actually using a mannequin. At the same time, it provides numerous creative insights and allows the exploration of a brand (as in our example) or a company or a program initiative. Moreover, the technique can easily be quantified as well because the order of stripping and dressing provides quantitative information in the form of an ordinal scale for judging the degree of importance of various elements.

The second tool—*"focusing and broadening"*—allows us to focus in and out on something. Think of the procedure as a zoom on your camera that can vary from a wide-angle lens to a telephoto. "Focusing and broadening" will allow you to see more details of the issue or to view it in terms of the big picture. You ask yourself the following questions: What happens when I focus in and out on the issue? What other elements come into view or are cropped out? Which ones should I consider; which ones should I ignore? What is the right lens through which to view this issue? The technique is similar to stripping and dressing in the sense that it focuses on essentials and nonessentials. However, there is also an important difference. In stripping and dressing, you are removing or adding things; here, things are brought into or out of view. For example, the technique can be very helpful to determine the right level of customer segmentation and targeting, ranging all the way from mass marketing to segment-of-one marketing.

The third creative exploration tool—*"exploring in a new context"*—removes the issue from its original context and applies a new context in a metaphorical way. To explore the public image of the organization, you may ask yourself—or customers—to imagine that the organization is going shopping, or to a karaoke party, or on an adventure trip. Where exactly would it go? What would it buy or sing or do? Who would come along? The technique is reminiscent of some of the projective devices used by market researchers (e.g., "If your product were an animal, what would it be?"). However, the situational/contextual metaphor is much more appropriate for many issues. Rather than assuming some static trait-like qualities, the contextual metaphor is much richer and allows for change by asking such questions as "Where else could the organization go; what else would it sing; what else would it do; under what circumstances would this happen?"

SUMMARY

The Blueprints of The Garage are broad-based, structural, and process-guided senior management initiatives. The Toolbox of The Garage consists of sets of specific tools that enable The Garage to be creative in every project. These tools include principles, methods, and techniques for engaging in individual and team creativity, e.g., working smoothly, and being well organized. The creative tension resolution tools and creative exploration tools are of particular importance because they can be used to unleash creativity in a variety of business domains.

The following three chapters focus on the Mastercrafts of The Garage.

the technology mastercraft

the branding mastercraft

the mastercraft of
customer experience management

the mastercrafts of the garage

They are *technology, branding,* and *customer experience management.* These Mastercrafts constitute the lifeblood of The Garage. They are cross-functional task forces: in each Mastercraft, the interplay of *bizz, buzz,* and *stuff* is critical. If utilized and applied the right way, the three Mastercrafts give life and energy to the organization, allowing it to develop corporate creativity to its fullest potential. The Mastercrafts need to be managed creatively in their own right by using the Blueprint and Toolbox. Then in turn they can enable and unleash creativity organization-wide and in each project.

WITH IT SAT ENTHRONED THE MASTERCRAFTS, WISEST OF THINGS

And the Contest of the Crafts was fierce.

But after rounds of intense battle, Technology, Branding, and Customer Experience Management were crowned as the Mastercrafts of The Garage.

Finance and Accounting stood ashamed on the sidelines.

Excerpts from *Garage-sagaen,* Book XI, verses 323–325, trans. Georg I. Skaander.

the technology of mastercraft

Technology is central to The Garage and therefore must be treated as a mastercraft. No company, regardless of industry, can afford not to keep pace with the dizzying rate of technological change. Everyone needs to be familiar with information and communication technology, in particular. Technology is thus essential for harnessing creativity in today's organizations.

Unfortunately, in addition to the digital divide between haves and have-nots, there is also a generational divide in terms of attitudes toward technologies and sophistication of usage. The following business parable borrows from the conventions of the detective story to explore these issues as a company changes . . . but not fast enough.

"Category Killer"

It was about seven-thirty in the morning, mid-November, with the sun not up yet and a brutal chill in the air. Art Langston had come into the of-

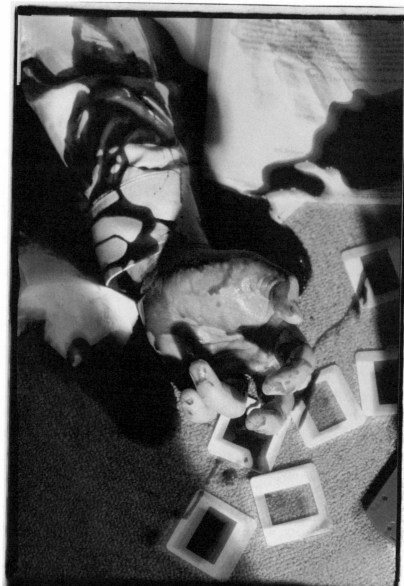

The blood was everywhere. It soaked the
young man's shirt and streaked his blond
hair. It spattered the papers and the
photographic slides that lay around the body
like fallen leaves.

fice early to join a conference call from Sydney. It was well before the assistants came in and fired up the computers and the photocopiers, before the young eager beavers came in and started blasting e-mails all over the planet. A sound from Glen's office stopped him, the loud and insistent sound of a telephone off the hook. Art went to investigate.

The blood was everywhere. It soaked the young man's shirt and streaked his blond hair. It spattered the papers and the photographic slides that lay around the body like fallen leaves. Bloody handprints streaked the desktop, skidded down the drawer fronts. Facedown, a curled fax adhered to the dark, sticky carpet.

Light from an overturned desk lamp cut across the carpet like a knife. It glinted off the gold clip of a pen that dug deeply into the man's swollen lower lip; the barrel of the pen disappeared into his mouth. Art drew a sharp breath. The pen was the same model as his own, black with a little white star on the cap. Art felt his breast pocket. The pen was still there.

He walked back to his office and watched himself dial 911.

Art and Glen hadn't always seen eye-to-eye. It was a technology-driven company; it had been for years. They had pioneered some of the earliest wireless communications technologies, and they prided themselves on bringing their customers the very latest innovations. Art had been with the company for twenty years. First as an engineer, then as a manager, he had overseen the development of the technology that would change the way people communicated. But his people had lately begun telling him that it wasn't enough.

"It's not just about technology, Art. Not anymore. It's about lifestyle," Glen had said in that earnest young way of his.

"No, I think in this market it's still about superior technology. Things are changing so fast—if we stay on the cutting edge of technology, we're competitive. We've gotta be."

"But, Art, we can't stay on the cutting edge if we look like a dinosaur. No one's even going to notice the technology if we look like this." Glen waved an expensive tri-fold brochure in the air. "It's ridiculous. This stuff is straight out of the eighties. The seventies, more like."

"You weren't even alive in the seventies," Art growled. "So, image is more important than quality? We can manufacture a piece of crap, but as long as we've got trendy marketing shit, people will buy it? They may

Strategy...

Corporate Planning is Customer Value

Everyone in a dark suit.
Everyone with that moronic, intensely
interested look on their face.
No one is like this anymore.

THE TECHNOLOGY OF MASTERCRAFT 95

buy it once, but how long do you think we'd survive after the thing falls apart in their hands?"

"Art, no, that's not what I'm saying. But you can't ignore the market. Our customers are young, and they're only gonna buy products that fit with their lifestyles. Just look at this user's manual—it's full of these posed corporate shots. Everyone in a dark suit. Everyone with that moronic, intensely interested look on their face. No one is like this anymore. Geez, it's embarrassing."

"God damn it, Glen!" Art was shouting now. "God *damn* it, Glen! You have no idea how much went into those pictures. You have no idea. Look at this thing! We went out of our way to make sure we had women, blacks, Asians, whatever. You know what this thing is? It's *diverse*. They wanted diversity, we gave them goddamn diversity. I don't know what the hell you're talking about, and you know something, I don't think you do, either."

"Listen, Art, I know what you're saying. But trust me, our customers won't see themselves in these shots, no matter how diverse they are. And if we don't give them something they connect with, then someone else will. Will you at least let me try?"

Art had let him try. Glen started pulling apart all the marketing materials. Every image, every word. He wanted to start again from scratch. He understood the technology. He was sincere as hell. And he seemed to understand what young consumers were looking for. It made Art feel old.

• • •

At approximately 0736 hours, 11/07/99, I responded to 19 State Street, 5th floor, regarding the victim of a homicide. Upon arrival, I noted the EMS had already arrived.

The victim was a male, white, approximately 30 years of age, later identified as Glen Wright. The victim was found on the floor of a small office. Upon entering the office, I noted the body was lying on the northern portion of the office floor, with its head in a northerly direction and its feet in a southerly direction. The victim's carotid artery appeared to have been punctured. Death probably occurred within moments, the victim having suffocated in his own blood. The apparent murder weapon, a fountain pen, was found inserted in the victim's mouth, its clip being af-

At approximately 0736 hours 11/07/99, I responded to 19 State Street, 5th floor, regarding the victim of a homicide. Upon arrival, I noted the EMS had already arrived.

fixed to the victim's lower lip. I searched the premises for any other potential weapon; however, this met with negative results.

I attempted to chalk the position of the victim's body; however, due to
the presence of a large amount of blood, this procedure was not completely successful.

A subject identified as Arthur Langston stated that he had come into
the office early and found the body. While waiting for the coroner to arrive, I questioned Langston about his relationship with the victim. At no
time did I question him about anything regarding the stabbing.

There were no fingerprints on the apparent murder weapon except
those of the decedent.

• • •

*Temping there just got to me. It was so much hypocrisy. At least temping at a
bank or insurance company or law firm—you know they're all full of shit and
they don't pretend not to be. All they want is the money and fuck everything
else. They don't pretend to be leading edge or cutting edge or bleeding edge or
whatever the hell they like to call themselves. I mean, they're assholes but at
least they're honest assholes, you know?*

*But that place was just so messed up. I just couldn't deal with it. And those
assholes just didn't get it. The stupid slogans and the fucking marketing stuff
was everywhere. Nothing but these stupid-looking white guys in suits. It made
me want to puke. So unbelievably cheesy.*

*And you know these assholes can't even use the Internet themselves. They
don't know HOW. It's incredible. They have their assistants find things for them,
and half the time they don't even know the stuff comes off the Web. They
hardly know what the Web is. What is that all about, anyway? A high-tech
company. Right! I built my own computer out of stuff I found, mainly. Had to
jack some memory off a machine at some law firm, but I'll bet they haven't
even noticed it's gone.*

• • •

"Jeanine, could you please print out my e-mails and bring them in?"

"They're already there, Mr. Castle."

"Oh, they are? Oh, Okay. Thanks. I thought those were the ones from
yesterday. Dammit. Jeanine, we're going to have to get some kind of filing

system for these things. There are so damn many of them, and they just pile up. Jesus, here's one from last Friday!"

"Maybe we shouldn't print them out, Mr. Castle. Maybe you could just answer them on the screen."

"No, that won't work. I think this whole Internet thing is more trouble than it's worth. Get me some kind of filing box or something, will you?"

"Sure, Mr. Castle. Do you want me to answer any of those e-mails from yesterday?"

"Yeah, sure, I'll get those to you later. They're still here, right? Yeah, okay. I'll get those to you."

• • •

Like one day I was there and I was dropping off a job with one of the old guy's assistants. And I have to like carry this shit up to her. They have an intranet, but the temps aren't allowed access to it—so I have to print all the shit out, save it on a floppy, take the elevator up six floors, and dump it on this chick's desk and wait for her to check to make sure her machine can read the damn floppy. How stupid is that? So like she's in the middle of a bidding war on eBay, so I just stand there watching her boss in his office trying to make a phone call. He picks up the land line on his desk. Then I see him actually flipping through a Rolodex. Then he remembers he's got the number on a fax. It's on that cheesy fax paper, the kind that when you write on it you get shivers down your spine, and the fucking fax paper keeps curling up so he can't read the number, and he's got the phone in one hand and he's trying to smooth out the fax with the other so he can read the number. And his phone cord is so tangled up and twisted around that it's gotten real short, so he has to kind of stoop down in order to get the phone to his ear when he's standing up. And I'm just standing there watching all this. These people are, like, the bleeding edge of mobile phone technology. It's hilarious.

• • •

"I'd be a lot happier if it'd been somebody else who'd found the body."

The detective curled forward in his chair. He looked as though his stomach hurt him. "So you say you got in at six, but there's nothing in the security log."

"I told you," Art said. "The guard was asleep. I was in a hurry to catch the call. I didn't stop to sign in."

And his phone cord is so tangled up and twisted around that it's gotten real short, so he has to kind of stoop down in order to get the phone to his ear when he's standing up. And these people are, like, the bleeding edge of mobile phone technology.

"Well, I wish to hell you had. It'd make my life a whole hell of a lot easier. Not that I think you did it. I don't. But here you are with a history of disagreements with the kid and arguments in front of your co-workers and so forth, and you just happen to be in the office early the morning he's murdered and no one sees you when you come in. Christ, doesn't anybody see anything around here?"

Art followed the investigation as closely as he could. After the first month, the calls from the detective began to taper off. There were no fingerprints, no suspects, no motives. None of the security videos showed anything unusual. Nothing at all turned up.

Glen's old office was renovated and turned into a copying and supply room. As the months wore on, Art became depressed. His doctor prescribed Zoloft. The company lost market share.

Then, eighteen months after the killing, the tech staff was doing a routine purging of files on the workstations in the temp area. Among the usual unofficial documents—résumés and cover letters, abortive screenplays, bad poetry—they had turned up an audio e-mail file. No one could figure out where it had come from or who had made it. The temps weren't supposed to have access to the Internet. It was not attached to any traceable e-mail account, but it was dated two nights after Glen's murder. It seemed to be a confession.

•   •   •

Anyhow I was there one night and I was really amped out. They asked me if I could work a double shift, because someone had a callback the next morning. So I said sure, okay. So it was really late and I was going on a break. They make you take a break, even if you don't want one. I mean like what the fuck are you supposed to do with a break at 4 o'clock in the morning in the business district? Even the security guy downstairs is sleeping half the time. It's like a ghost town down there; IT IS DEAD. Everything was closed, and it was unbelievably cold and windy. I'd rather just work through and leave early, but of course they don't let you do that—you have to take a break. So I figure whatever, at least I'll get out of the friggin building. I put on my coat and gloves and I'm going down the stairs, cuz the elevators all have those security cameras and they skeev me out. I can't deal with it. So for some reason I came out on five, and I walk by this office. And here's this idiot in a white shirt and tie—at 4 fucking a.m. It's a guy I've never seen before, blond and kind of young. And he's got all these photos and slides and brochures and stuff all over his desk. Unbelievably cheesy stuff. You wouldn't believe the pile of shit he had.

So anyhow, I see this picture of my friend Kwanda—she's doing this really cool online education thing now, but she told me she used to do some modeling. And there she is in this totally cheesy picture, in this gray suit with this old guy, and they're both, like, staring at a computer screen—it looks like a fucking 386—and he's pointing at the screen and they're both trying to look really in-ter-es-ted. And they've got her hair all slick and her makeup is ridiculous and she's wearing a string of pearls. I've never seen her look like that—I almost didn't recognize her. It was like, "Who are you and what have you done with Kwanda?"

And I just lost it. I mean, I just got so pissed off. I saw this cheesy pen on the guy's desk—those big black and white ones like they all have—and I just lost it.

• • •

No one recognized the voice on the audio file. The woman who had been the night word processing supervisor at the time of the murder had been downsized, her job function taken over by a temp. It took three weeks to trace her to St. Paul, Minnesota. It took another week to learn that she had been killed when her right front tire disintegrated on the Interstate one icy night.

Human resources kept only paper files on temporary workers. But the relevant ones were old by now, and the HR director said they had definitely been shipped to storage on the south side of the city. Paper files were kept for two months after an employee left, then sent to the warehouse.

Art went to the south side with the detective to look for the files. The warehouse was in an old industrial district. Red brick factories, long since abandoned, lined the deserted streets. Parking lots were guarded by rusty chain-link fences, empty except for the weeds pushing up through the asphalt. A brick smokestack, its factory demolished long ago, stood alone and silent. The names of forgotten companies—Anderson Textiles, Hollister Paper Company, Ajax Agate Glass Marble Co., Inc.—crumbled on worn marble slabs above the boarded-up doorways. High on the buildings hung faded FOR RENT signs, visible from the elevated railway that divided the district from the rest of the city.

Inside, the warehouse was lit by harsh overhead fluorescents emitting a

Temping there just got to me....
And I just lost it.

low, constant hum. Along the high bare walls stood rows of mismatched five-drawer filing cabinets. A filing clerk leaned against the counter, eating pork and rice out of a takeout container. He was a tall, pale man, with black stringy hair that fell over his collar. His ample waist tapered to narrow shoulders and an almost pointed head. His white fingers were plump and moist-looking.

The clerk made the detective fill out a request in pencil, then studied the form closely for several moments. "Let's see now. What's the date you're after?" He looked up at them in quiet triumph. "Nope," he said. "Recycled. We only keep records like this for six months. Then we recycle 'em."

The clerk wiped his fingers with a thin paper napkin. From outside the building came the steady beeping sound of a truck backing up. The fluorescent lights hummed.

WHAT DOES THE BUSINESS PARABLE MEAN?

"Change or die." Business publications and consultants adopted the phrase as a mantra. Change or die. And yet it's not that simple. What does it mean to change? Usually, it is said that technology has a key role to play in this transformation. But technology is changing all the time; how far is your organization supposed to go with it?

One point this grim little story makes is that it's not enough simply to *have* these technologies. You have to use them well. Technologies have the capability to transform businesses, but they can only do so when used intelligently. When companies make these new technologies available but employees resist them—when people insist on printing out their e-mails, for example—then they are not making intelligent use of these technologies to improve their operations.

It's more than a problem with internal efficiency, though. It's also a question of staying in touch with the rest of the world. At times of rapid change, companies have to work extra hard to keep up, not just with their competition but also with their customers. This parable presents a company that is so absorbed in its *stuff*—its superior telecommunications technology—that it neglects *the buzz* all around it—the lifestyles of its customers.

In this story, the murderer inadvertently kills the one person in the organization who was most committed to change. The murderer doesn't know that. Nihilistic, perhaps, but the market is ruthless and undiscriminating. It doesn't care how hard you're trying—it cares only for results. Sometimes the wrong companies die. Don't let yours be one of them.

TECHNOLOGY AS A MASTERCRAFT

Starting in the mid-nineties, revolutionary new communications technologies began to make inroads into our daily workstyles and lifestyles. These technologies have made companies more efficient and effective. They have improved the information flow within the organization and between the company and its customers and suppliers. The right use of this technology is a key element of creating competitive advantage. Therefore The Garage must make technology one of its Mastercrafts, i.e., provide employees with the newest technology and make sure it gets used organization-wide to harness creativity and innovation.

In the long list of communications technologies that have affected our work lives, two stand out: the Internet and mobile communications. Because of the Internet and mobile communications, we can be constantly informed and continuously reachable. Soon, we and the intelligent devices around us (such as our TVs, refrigerators, and toasters) will be constantly online and ready to receive and exchange all sorts of information in all sorts of formats.

The Internet has changed many people's lives. The Web offers a world of information. It also offers cost savings and efficiency, thus increasing velocity in supply-chain management. Consumers have instant access to books, CDs, and other goods, which are delivered right to their doorsteps. Ordinary transactions are made much easier. With a few clicks, consumers can book a flight and the lodging and rental car to go with it, and via mobile access, they can do so while they are in transit.

To illustrate the immense opportunities associated with the Internet and mobile communication, let's revisit a company and service featured in chapter 1, NTT DoCoMo's i-mode. Put out by Japan's largest mobile telecommunications provider, i-mode offers consumers continuous access to the Internet through their mobile phones. Personal users can access a wide range of interactive online services, including banking, news and stock updates, telephone directory services, ticket reservations, online book sales, restaurant reservations, instant e-mail, and much more. i-mode is also being fitted for a range of future business uses, including data exchanges between field representatives and headquarters. The service has been a tremendous success in Japan, attracting new users at the rate of 50,000 *per day*. Moreover, it has provided a revenue stream for numerous content providers. Telecommunications providers in other countries throughout the world are looking to i-mode as a model for their own product development.

USING TECHNOLOGY CREATIVELY

Communications, customer relations, product launches, services, and other dealings with customers will be increasingly shaped by technology. Therefore, any organization must use technology *creatively* in its dealings with its business customers and with end consumers.

But using technology creatively is still a very difficult notion for many companies to grasp. Most businesspeople's attitude toward technology is "We've got to use this because everyone else is, but we really don't get it." This attitude is understandable. Technology has been changing so fast that average users almost feel defeated before they start. What's more, technologies can represent a hidden threat: applications are sometimes plagued by hidden bugs that aren't diagnosed until it is "too late." For many businesses, technology remains a bit of a mystery—something for the IT department to manage and keep out of everybody else's hair.

But this attitude has to change—in every business, in every industry. It has to change because it keeps companies from exploiting the full benefits of technology. It also prevents them from using technology creatively to build and transform their businesses. In fact, most companies still only scratch the surface of what they could be accomplishing through the technology currently available to them.

Take an insurance company as an example. It's hardly a sexy industry or cutting-edge business, but let's look at how the creative use of technology might transform it. Imagine that somebody has had a car accident and gets in touch with their insurance company to ask for help. This insurance company now has a wide variety of opportunities to add value through technology. People are upset after accidents—what if the insurance company's Web site included step-by-step guidance about what to do following an accident, so that customers wouldn't worry that they've forgotten something? What if the Web site could also hook the customer up with a car rental company? And what if it could provide a list of reputable repair shops in the customer's area? If the customer was injured in the accident, what if the Web site had a special section explaining what kinds of documentation the company needs from the hospital and/or doctor? Better yet, what if the Web site allowed the doctor and the customer to file their claims online? What if accessing this Web site and putting in a code (via a mobile device) was the only thing a customer had to do to get the problem resolved?

If an insurance company could do all of this well, it could become a true partner to customers in a time of crisis rather than just another bureaucracy to hassle with in a long and unpleasant process. Calling the insurance company could be a comforting experience rather than a frustrating one. An insurance company that can do this offers peace of mind and thus strengthens its brand. Of course, the other players involved in this situation—the car manufacturer, the service station, the car rental company, the hospital—can add value of their own. These companies can also work together in an alliance in which every company has access to the critical information to serve the customer well—not by passing around bureaucratic documents, but as part of a networked service.

As this example suggests, creative use of technology can reshape entire industries. It provides an opportunity for companies to redefine themselves. It can totally transform what companies can offer their customers.

Given this powerful potential, an organization that aspires to be a garage needs to make the creative use of technology and the Internet a Mastercraft. In this chapter, we first focus on how technology can be used creatively in organizational facilities and workplaces. Next, we focus on the knowledge and resources that are required to mastercraft Web sites. We then turn to a discussion of how to mastercraft the entire supply chain in which the company participates.

HOW FACILITIES AND WORKPLACES ARE CHANGING

Our traditional workstyle throughout the nineteenth and twentieth centuries—since the Industrial Revolution and through the period of the administrator, manager, and service worker—has been to leave the house in the morning and to go to a plant or an office. Prior to the Industrial Revolution, when many people worked at home—on a family farm or in a small shop attached to the house—the workplace was close at hand. In the age of mass production, the workplace became larger and more complex, housing a host of tangible facilities: both machinery and files, either paper or tape. Industrial Age workers were thus forced to go to the workplace.

Today, the workplace has become largely electronic. There has been a massive shift in hardware—in terms of what we use and where we use it. First, many workers are now able to take their workplace wherever they go. The workplace itself has become mobile because its key hardware and information reside on a laptop, on another mobile device, or perhaps even on a Web site. Now the workplace is everywhere, and we can always get what we need to get our work done. We no longer have to go to work—we take work with us.

This new mobility will have a major impact not just in terms of where employees work but also in terms of how they work—both alone and with others. The new technology has enabled a myriad of creative options in the way people may work together, and crucial choice for the productivity of an organization. However, these creative options are available only if everyone knows how to use the technology. In The Garage, everyone must achieve a certain standard of technological versatility. There is no excuse for not knowing how to process e-mails, find information online, or work with networked resources. Whether they know it or not, executives who delegate this knowledge to their assistants and ignore it themselves are slowly but surely rendering themselves obsolete. No one is "too senior" or "too strategically focused" to get their hands dirty with technology.

With these ideas in mind, let's examine what developments are likely to come in the years ahead and how they can increase the productivity of organizations that can use them creatively.

First, efficient communication and data transfer across devices will become the norm. Right now, you are likely to have different software on different devices (mobile phones, portable devices, the laptop and desktop), and these different software products cannot communicate with each other, or at least not efficiently. This will change when XML (extensible mark-up language) becomes standard. Through XML, any smart device can communicate with any other easily. The organization must be ready to embrace this opportunity to streamline business and the work-lives of its employees.

Second, integration across programs and across functions will increase dramatically. When you work now, you have to move in and out of programs, and to share information across various programs you engage in lots of duplication. This situation is going to change with new software both at the individual and at the firm level that will allow greater integration.

Consider, for example, the value of integration in mobile technical service work. With a wearable mobile computing device, service personnel can instantly call up a map of the piece of equipment they are servicing. They can send a snapshot with a digital camera or a streaming video back to their headquarters. They can report back when the job is done. They can file a notification report, indicating when the damage was repaired, which parts were used, what the cause of damage was—all in real time. They can do the accounting right then and there and indicate the billing for these parts. Can you imagine the efficiencies and new value that can be created through such processes?

Third, software upgrades will be quick and easy. Right now, if you want to get new software, you have to buy it and have it installed on your system. New versions of the software become available every few months, and you may or may not choose to buy and install the upgrade. This state of affairs will change. More and more software, whether for end users or business users, will be available on the Internet—ready to be configured, upgraded, paid for, and used on the fly. Can you imagine how easy it will be to communicate within the organization and with partners when everyone can access the same programs anywhere and any time? And no one says to you, "I can't read your file, is there any way you could send it to me in version 4.2?"

Fourth, right now, most of the information you access is not personalized. The devices that you are using may know a little bit about you (e.g., your name and password). But they usually cannot recognize your voice; they cannot assist you in a personalized way. This will change as new interfaces are developed. In the future, using a keyboard as an interface may become the exception rather than the rule. For example, future interfaces may include audio for browsing, especially on mobile phones and personal digital assistants or a combination of video and audio. Imagine what it will do to business when we can interact with intelligent devices in a more natural way.

Finally, business and personal computing are still somewhat separated. For several years now, end consumers have used mobile communication devices like Palm, Psion, or Hewlett-Packard Organizers to manage their lives; they have calendars, to-do lists, memos, and databases. More sophisticated users have added programs (games, alarm clocks, pictures, enhanced calculators) and synchronized their organizers with their mobile phones or watches. Even more sophisticated users may be subscribing to online services which they add to the device in a wireless fashion. These add-ons allow subscriptions to online editions of publications like *The Economist*, the *Wall Street Journal*, or *Salon*. They also allow users to receive movie schedules per Zip code and to make restaurant reservations. The next step is to integrate the mobile devices like these and the NTT DoCoMo i-mode service, which have been used primarily for personal computing, into mainstream business software. Can you imagine what this kind of capability could do for your sales and customer relations?

But it's not just a matter of imagination. These changes are not some science fiction futurecast; they're happening right now and may become standard soon. Therefore, companies must be ready to mastercraft these new technologies to capitalize on the opportunities that they offer to business.

MASTERCRAFTING COMMUNICATIONS TECHNOLOGIES NOW

The old approach to adopting new technologies—that is to say, slowly and unimaginatively—simply won't do. What companies need to do is to prepare for these new technologies, and once they are here, make creative use of them as quickly as possible. Most companies are too passive, too unimaginative in using technology in the workplace. Second only to employees' brainpower, technology is the single most important factor in workplace productivity. It represents a hugely exciting area for innovation and creativity.

What is to be done? We suggest you immediately get up to date on what technology is available, and what is coming soon. Then launch an initiative to find out how you can make use of these new technologies in various projects. Then integrate these plans throughout the entire company: develop a timetable for making them available in your organization; develop a learning program that allows everyone to become informed about their potential for the company and for their particular job function; put together diverse groups to develop future scenarios on how to structure the workplace in your company. In these initiatives the concepts of dialectics, balancing, and alternation, first introduced in chapter 2, and the corresponding tools discussed in chapter 3—creative synthesis, creative balancing, creative oscillation—will be very useful.

When Boeing develops a new plane, it works closely with the major airlines, examining a wide variety of issues from safety to passenger comfort to ease of use by the crew. An airplane is an expensive and important product, and customer input is key to its development. The same process should occur in the development of new hardware and software. Developers need to work much more closely with the users and the dreamers who can provide input from an entirely different perspective. Rather than passively accepting the latest version of whatever, users need to play an active role in the development of new technology. Otherwise, we will continue to be held hostage by companies whose products may not meet our needs.

Now let's turn to mastercrafting the company's Web site.

MASTERCRAFTING THE COMPANY WEB SITE

In today's business environment, the company's Web site is its single most significant public presence. By now, the Web site is more important than the company's building, more important than its glossy brochures, and more important than its advertising. The site creates a first impression, it represents the organization, and it presents a huge opportunity to provide

information, interact with customers, get new product ideas, provide service, promote products, and actually sell products. Nothing else in the history of commerce has been as versatile a tool.

A company's Web site represents the crucial intersection of its *bizz,* its
stuff, and its *buzz. The bizz:* Nowhere is structure, logic, and functionality
more important than on a company's Web site. Willingly or not, a company exposes its inner self on its site. Remember the old wisdom that says
if you want to know how clean a restaurant's kitchen is, you should look
at its restrooms? If your Web site is poorly organized, full of bugs, and
hard to navigate, consumers are likely to form the same impression of the
company as a whole. *The buzz* is important, too. Your office may have the
best *buzz* in the world, but if your Web site lacks energy, excitement, and
personality, visitors won't stay long, and they won't come back. Finally,
there is *the stuff.* As more and more commerce and other interactions
move onto the Web, it will be critical to win customers' trust by providing
them with information and services, as well as products, via the Internet.
The Web site is where you have to get it right. All of it. That's why you
need to mastercraft your site.

By now, many companies have constructed their third- or fourth-
generation Web sites. And still many are failing to deliver. Let's have a
look at what's out there on the Net.

Some companies' sites look like little more than scanned-in corporate
reports or product brochures. These "corporate brochure sites" are text-
and information-heavy, and they are painfully boring. Such content-laden
sites are in fact inappropriate for the medium of the Web. They do not
take advantage of the Web's unique strengths: the interlinked nature of
many sites that invites browsing, the interactivity with the user, and the
opportunity to customize the site for the user.

Just as bad is the opposite extreme: the "oh-so-webby" site. These sites
are full of animation and sound (designed using the latest "Flash" technology); they are long on bells-and-whistles but short on information
value. They require lengthy download times and all the latest plug-ins
that many users do not have and will not bother to install.

And then there is the transaction-oriented, functional e-commerce site.
Many of these e-commerce sites fail to deliver on what is supposed to be
their core essence: an efficient transaction. Too often, customers have to

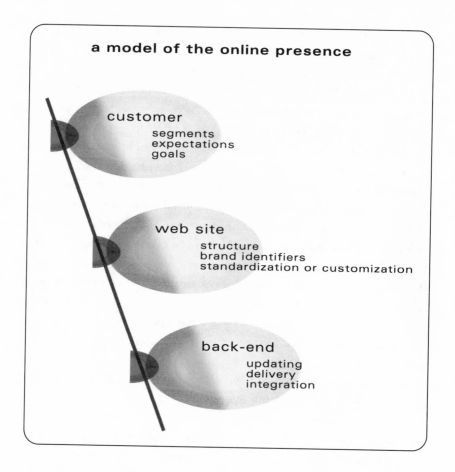

a model of the online presence

customer
    segments
    expectations
    goals

web site
    structure
    brand identifiers
    standardization or customization

back-end
    updating
    delivery
    integration

click forever to get to the merchandise, and once they find it, they cannot make much sense of the tiny static pictures that are provided. Often, these sites don't work as well as they should. Most annoyingly, poor back-end support means that merchandise often arrives late or not at all, and the problem gets even worse during the times when the customer needs the product most, such as Christmas time.

Now let's take a look at what it takes to mastercraft the site. Here is a framework for generating creative (useful and original) Web sites. In addition to the right facilities (servers, routers, and other infrastructural components), this requires a lot of knowledge and resources regarding understanding the front end (i.e., the customers), the site itself, and back-end support. Moreover, a creative site must be the joint product of marketing and sales, the Web designers, the IT group, and senior management—and it must receive input from anyone in the organization with insights to contribute.

Mastercrafting the Front End: The Customer Interface

Mastercrafting the front end means that you, as a whole company, understand who your customers are, what they expect from your site, and what their goals are—and that you use this understanding to design your site accordingly.

To create a dynamite site, we first need to decide which "e-customers" to target. In this regard, geographic, demographic, or lifestyle segmentation (in business-to-consumer markets) as well as industrial segmentation (in business-to-business markets) can be useful; yet, as Forrester Research has found, attitude toward technology (pessimistic vs. optimistic) and the primary motivation for using technology (career, family, entertainment) are often better segmentation variables.[14] Web segmentation profiles are now widely available from firms such as Forrester Research, Roper Starch, Jupiter Communications, Scarborough Research, and others. This information can also be easily accessed on Web research sites.

However, these broadly based customer data about new technologies need to be supplemented with an understanding of how users actually approach a given site. SCHMITT has conducted extensive research on this issue with a graduate student, Reimar Mueller. He found that the customers' expectations and user goals greatly affect online behavior and a site's "stickiness," including the probability of liking the site, browsing it, and bookmarking it.

The research also showed that customer expectations about a Web site are often created by a general knowledge of the company. Just imagine, for example, what kind of site you might expect from a company like American Express or Starbucks—what kind of look and feel, what kind of information. Moreover, a company's advertising styles can also set up expectations for their Web presence. When Visa, for instance, has an aggressive ad for its new "Next Card," declaring that "Banks are History," we expect a cutting-edge site to match the iconoclasm of the ad campaign. When we actually visit these sites, we may be positively impressed or we may be disappointed. The expectations consumers bring to a site affect their online behavior.

Goals are another important determinant of online behavior. To put it simply, is the customer's goal to seek content, to engage in a transaction, or perhaps to be entertained? The www.cnn.com site gets huge traffic every day, but people stay for only a short period to get quick news updates. By contrast, users go to the *Encyclopaedia Britannica* (www.britannica.com) site to gather in-depth intelligence and knowledge (e.g., to get answers to question such as What is creativity?, as we did in Chapter 1). It is important to understand these different goals when designing navigation structures, putting up search engines, and planning hyperlinks with other sites. Similarly, on an e-commerce site, does the user want to shop with one click or browse around awhile before buying? Understanding user goals can help companies create satisfying online experiences for them.

Mastercrafting the Design of the Web Site

The second key consideration is the type of site that is needed. First and foremost, a Web site needs to have the appropriate functional components: transparent site structure; easy navigation tools; and appropriate information exchange systems. However, a site also needs noticeable and differentiated brand identifiers such as a memorable URL and the right corporate brand symbols (site logos, buttons, and other brand icons). For years, the amazon.com Web site has exceeded other sites, in terms of both functionality and branding, and has been nominated by Forrester Research and other companies as the best Web site in various categories (movies, books, music).

Moreover, we need to be creative over the issue of standardization and customization. Let us illustrate the choice by examining two Web sites more closely: www.sephora.com, owned by LVMH, the French luxury products conglomerate; and www.reflect.com, owned by Procter & Gamble.

Sephora primarily uses a standardization approach. The site sells major cosmetics brands, and these brands are not customized. In contrast, reflect.com's goal is to "create one-of-a-kind beauty products inspired by your individuality." When customers first approached the site in the spring of 2000, they were told: "Please take a minute and answer a few questions that will help our beauty experts personalize a web site for you. Help us get to know you better by telling us about your desires, your needs, your lifestyle and your beauty sense." Many of these questions are playful and creative, such as what consumers like to wear, what animal they would choose to be, what images they find most visually appealing. Based on that information, the site learns general aesthetic preferences, but the customer remains free to alter subsequent suggestions offered by the site. At the end, customers create their own products including product ingredients, packaging, and messages. This choice between standardization and customization needs to be faced in every industry.

Mastercrafting the Back End

The final factor is the back-end support system. From a technology perspective, it includes the management of the overall site architecture (e.g., of routers and connectivity tools), the database, payment systems, transaction or credit card verification system, and other technological tools needed to manage the site—which is very much a matter of knowledge and skills.

But setting up a satisfactory Web site is not a pure technology issue; it also requires design, marketing, and management resources. Moreover, beyond the construction and setup, there is the day-to-day management issue of the site, which again requires all different sorts of knowledge and skills. Three issues are key: *updates, delivery,* and *integration with other communications.* Updates are necessary to accommodate new customers, new information, and new technologies. Updates are thus part of the continuous improvement process online, and are especially critical for content-heavy sites. Delivery is a key part of any selling effort. Finally, managers need to set up the right communication structures to blend Web communications with other sorts of communications. The Web site and the online experience it provides are not a stand-alone marketing and communications tool but rather part of a company's comprehensive communications strategies (including visual/verbal identity, PR, advertising, sales visits, etc.). The best companies speak with one voice, integrating the virtual and the real.

As with the workplace, it is worthwhile to examine future developments that will affect a company site. Currently, most users access the Web using a modem of limited speed. This is likely to change in the very near future. Thus, one future scenario to consider is of a world with broadband high-speed Internet access. In such a world, many of the current technological restrictions on Internet branding will no longer exist. Customers will be able to access video and audio information easily, and not only in the form of animationlike "Flash" files. Video paired with audio will be as common as in TV commercials. Picture and sound quality will drastically improve. Software that already exists for digital touch and smell can be put to use. As a result, the Web will become much less text-heavy and will provide a truly multisensory experience. And these changes are coming fast. So, how should your Web site then change? This question must be addressed through continuous rounds of mastercrafting.

Another future scenario concerns mobile rather than stationary access. Most users today access the Web via a stationary device (a desktop or laptop computer). In the near future, accessing the Internet via a hand-held personal computing device (such as an electronic organizer, telephone, or watch), paired with GPS (Global Positioning Systems), will allow companies to send localized messages (e.g., when customers are in stores). At the same time, though, the new interface (a small screen compared to the typical laptop or desktop screen) will put limitations on the multisensory marketing that is likely to be the result of broadband. The challenge for designers and marketers will then be to design situation- and customer-specific sites for different situations and customer needs. What opportunities do you see for your business?

MASTERCRAFTING SUPPLY-CHAIN MANAGEMENT

This is how supply-chain management traditionally works: a supplier ships raw material to the manufacturer; the manufacturer adds value by producing a product and ships it to a distributor; the distributor ships it to a wholesaler; the wholesaler ships the product to the retailer; and the customer buys it from the store.

There are billions of dollars of inefficiencies in every supply-chain management system in various forms. One inefficiency occurs when too much merchandise is stored in inventory. Another inefficiency occurs when the merchandise is back-logged. Information flow from the cus-

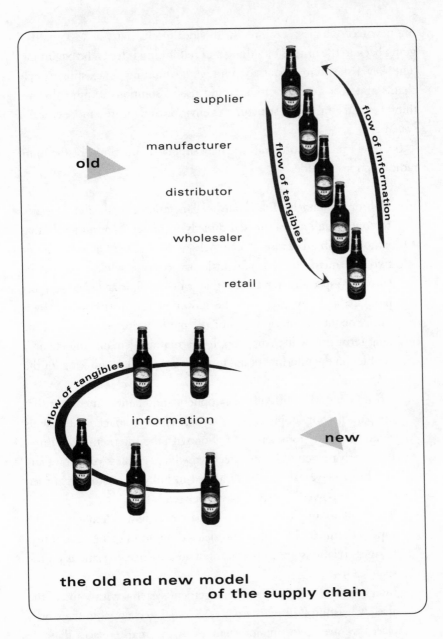

old

supplier

manufacturer

distributor

wholesaler

retail

flow of tangibles

flow of information

new

flow of tangibles

information

**the old and new model
of the supply chain**

tomer back to the manufacturer and the raw materials supplier is often inefficient. If one component is not supplied or if the wrong one is supplied, the system may come to a standstill.

So, how can organizations redesign their supply chain creatively using new technologies? Let's revisit the idea of creativity as "originality," going back to the origins of a thing and rethinking it from the beginning. The key issue here is not to limit your thinking to existing supply chains and cost savings. Original and useful solutions require that we think beyond established structures to envision and create a more efficient system.

So, how can we mastercraft the new supply chain? Some of the more radical options include:

- Cut out channels. For many organizations, with the Internet, the opportunity arises to sell directly to the end consumer. If that is not possible because of channel conflict, usually at least one or two intermediaries that add little or no value whatsoever can be cut out, especially for goods that can be digitized. For a short period, they may still have the power of the distribution system (think about the music stores or the publishing houses), but in the long term this will change. So, it is a matter of managing channel conflicts in the interim but not forgetting the radical thinking for the long term.
- Create networks with all the suppliers and channel members that are part of your supply chain. Your enterprise management systems should be ready for open integration with the Internet. Don't think that a private network can succeed any longer unless your company is a huge player and can still afford to bully its customers. (Even then, your power is likely to be challenged.)
- Think of a supply chain as a dynamic system. Members of the supply chain can be added and deleted on an ongoing basis. Sure, business relations are important, but so are virtual relations on the spot.
- Integrate your supply-chain management systems with some of the already existing B2B marketplaces. Parallel to changes in the workplace, we are seeing major changes in the marketplaces that we access both as consumers and as industrial buyers. In these marketplaces, everyone will interact in real time with anybody in a "co-opetitive" fashion.
- Most important, think of the supply chain no longer as a "chain" but

as a "circle," where products respond to accessible market information in the center. That way, you will turn the supply chain into a customer-linked rather than an organization-routed concept.

SUMMARY

In this chapter, we showed how creative use of technology can add new value to the organization and its customers. To unleash that value, garagelike organizations are beginning to restructure their facilities and workplaces and are mastercrafting their Web sites and their supply-chain management systems. Technology is a great enabler of creativity, and if managed with the right *bizz, buzz,* and *stuff,* may even provide a lasting competitive advantage.

In the next chapter, we turn to the issue of *branding.* As we will see, branding the company, divisions, and projects is key for unleashing creativity. Branding has emerged as a key management idea for any organization and has been in the focus of organizations' attention for the last ten years. So it may seem that there isn't much else to say about it. This is not true. In The Garage, branding is a Mastercraft, bringing together *the bizz, the buzz,* and *the stuff* to define the soul of the organization.

the branding mastercraft

Despite all the hype about branding, companies have really only just begun to understand its potential and its implications. Branding has traditionally been viewed as an external projection device through which a company communicates with the outside world. In this view, branding is about names, logos and advertising, and about awareness and image management. As a result, it is rarely intimately related to organizational values and practices. The following business parable "love story" makes it clear that branding must be more—it must be treated as a mastercraft, which means that the inside of the organization and the image we project on the outside are creatively aligned. As we follow the passionate love story between a fiery marketing vice president and a shy branding consultant, we also trace the conflict between the old school of branding and the new view advocated in this chapter.

"Knowing Susan . . ."

Susan sat pensively at her desk, her delicate hand absently smoothing the soft brown hair that fell in waves to her shoulders. Her pale, warm skin

𝒯he business cards were all hers,
all from the bank, each with a different
logo printed on a different card stock.

was set off by a delft blue silk blouse; a gold locket graced her long neck. On her desk sat the newest and most powerful PC available, with a cradle for her Palm Top. Next to the computer stood a small vase of flowers, brought in fresh by Susan every Monday morning. To see Susan in this artistic pose, it would have been hard to imagine that she was senior vice president of marketing of multinational giant QuantaBank, and one of the corporation's brightest lights.

"Hi, Sue!" The strong, masculine voice suddenly announced itself from her open doorway. Brilliant white teeth glinted in a confident smile. Greg Musk was a tall man, with broad shoulders and deep green eyes—as he liked to say, the color of money.

He was also the bank's director of marketing and Susan's immediate boss. Office gossip had frequently linked Susan and Greg in a romantic affair, but nothing of the kind had ever happened. It was not for want of trying, at least on his part. It seemed to Susan that when he wasn't trying to impress her, he was talking as if she were already his. *How can he act that way,* Susan often wondered, *when he really has no idea who I am—who I really am—and never even tries to find out? And here I know so well what makes him tick . . .*

"I got a voice mail from that corporate identity guy," Greg said. "He says he'll be here in about fifteen minutes."

"That's wonderful," Susan replied. "I can't wait to get started on this project with him. I think this will finally give us the competitive edge we need."

Greg's face reddened slightly, and Susan could tell he was angry. *Oh no,* she thought, *I was too direct again.* Greg didn't like this business of bringing in consultants to do what he felt was his job. And he damned well didn't like Susan showing enthusiasm about it. "Well, we'll just have to see how he does," Greg snapped. "The key to all of this is understanding the brand, Susan, and if he can't do that, he won't be around here for too long. He'll just be another consultant out on his ass." Greg let a moment pass, then added pointedly, "Plus, Susan, we can do that job ourselves, you and me." Without letting her answer, he turned and disappeared around the corner.

Susan sighed and turned back to her computer screen. The fact was that the bank's brand was in tatters. Too many mergers and too many designers had left behind a trail of mutant logos, typefaces, and color schemes. Susan herself sometimes had trouble remembering which logo the company was currently using. She had carried mountains of old letterhead home to give to her sister's children to draw on. She had recycled boxes of envelopes.

"Susie!" Greg's voice made her jump. "This is Mark Rosen, from bisonandbass. Mark's going to be working with us on the corporate branding project. Mark, this is Susan Venner."

"I'm so happy to meet you, Mark." Susan reached out. She had constant pain in her right hand from using her mouse, and she had come to dread handshakes, especially with men who thought a crushing grip made a good impression. She braced herself, made eye contact, and smiled. Mark's hand was warm and dry, his grip gentle. She almost hated to let go. "Hi, Susan," he said, "I'm glad to know you."

"Mark tells me he worked on rebranding Mason," said Greg.

"Did you really?" she enthused. "That was great work! They look terrific."

"Exactly," said Greg decisively. Susan hoped he would not be too aggressive.

"Thank you," Mark replied, in a voice that was soft, yet rich and full. "It was fun—they're really good people to work with, really open and creative." Mark looked Susan straight in the eye as he spoke to her. His gaze was intimate, but at the same time respectful—not proprietary or threatening. There was something almost frightening about the honesty that shone from his eyes.

Greg cut in. "I thought we could all have a few minutes of face time, and then I'll let you two go at it."

The three sat down and Greg began lecturing Mark about the company's branding history. Susan watched Mark carefully. She could almost see him thinking. He listened intently, and a gentle light flickered in his grey eyes. When he asked questions, his voice was soft and thoughtful.

Then suddenly the meeting was over. "All right, great," Greg said, his tone of voice commanding and final. "Here's to the new QuantaBank brand. Susie knows that I have some ideas of my own about the corporate brand, but I'll keep those to myself. I'd really like to hear what you kids come up with. So you'll work with Susie, and Susie will report to me. It's a pleasure to meet you, Mark." He flashed a smile, and his gold cufflinks gleamed as he left the office.

Greg's abrupt departure left Susan and Mark flat-footed and silent for a moment. Was he trying to suppress a laugh? she wondered. She half hoped that he was, but at the same time she knew he would be too professional to show it.

Susan broke the silence: "I have something I want to show you." Opening her drawer, she pulled out an envelope, from which she drew six business cards. She laid them out carefully and deliberately on the desk, like a woman turning over a winning poker hand. The business cards were all hers, all from the bank, each with a different logo printed on a different card stock. A smile began to flicker across Mark's face, starting first in his eyes, then warming all his features. "These are just from the past two years," she said. "This one is from my posting in London—they've got an entirely different logo over there. I have this fantasy of framing all of these and displaying them in the office—a sort of work-in-progress exhibition. But I don't think Greg would see the humor in it."

They both laughed. His laugh was warm and full. It was like laughing with an old friend.

Arranging the cards on her desk, Mark smiled as he said, "You guys are a mess."

"Not really," Susan replied confidently. "We're really pretty good, but nobody would know it from the way we present ourselves."

"Okay, you just *look* like a mess," he replied, laughing. He raised his eyes to hers. "I mean, not you personally."

A moment passed.

"These cards are great," Mark said, breaking the silence; "can I take them? Just for now. I promise I'll give them back, but I'd like to keep them around for inspiration."

"Sure, help yourself. It's nice to think of myself as an inspiration."

"Our fundamental approach to branding begins by looking at a company as though it were a person," Mark began. "Your customers are people, and people relate to other people, not to big aggressive faceless monsters. At least they relate *better* to other people than to big aggressive faceless monsters. Generally speaking, of course. You see what I mean?"

"Absolutely."

*H*e had some business cards
spread out on the table in front of him.... He was
writing something on the back of one of them.

Mark looked thoughtful. "So we have to look deeper—at the core. We need to find out what's positive about the organization, and use this as a model for everything else. It looks like my job is to find the absolute best." He held her gaze for a moment, and then smiled. "I'm really looking forward to this, Susan."

They shook hands again as he left. Unbidden, a scene from Susan's favorite opera, *La Bohème,* burst into her mind: when the two lovers meet for the first time, and search for the key in the dark, and they touch hands and the tenor sings, "Oh, what tender hands." After Mark left, she sat quietly for several moments. She was going to enjoy working with him.

• • •

Susan didn't see a lot of Mark for the next week or so. He did stop by her office every morning, and often brought her a cup of coffee and talked to her about the research he was doing. He frequently asked for her advice, and seemed genuinely to value her opinion. But most of his days were spent talking to other people in the organization. He wanted to talk to everyone, it seemed! He met with the financial analysts; he ate lunch with the customer service managers; he interviewed HR specialists. One day in the cafeteria Susan overheard a young administrative assistant telling her friend about "that cute new guy in marketing." She was surprised at the pang of jealousy she felt.

Then suddenly one morning Mark appeared in Susan's doorway, a boyish smile on his face. He reached with both arms to the top of the doorjamb and hung from it, doing a couple of halfhearted pull-ups.

"You're going to break it," she smiled.

Dropping lithely to the floor, he said, "Let's go to the bank."

"What?"

"It's almost lunchtime, right? Let's go to the bank. You know, do some field research. See this bank in action."

"Well," she hesitated. She had a report to finish and an inbox of e-mails to answer. *But* . . . "Why not?" she said.

On the way out, Susan poked her head into Greg's office. "Mark and I are going to visit some of the branches. I'll be back in a couple of hours." Greg stared. He opened his mouth, but nothing came out. Susan turned and left.

They spent the afternoon going from one bank branch to another—six in all—gathering information, forming impressions. At one branch they pretended they were opening a coffee shop and asked about small business loans. At another they said they were getting married and asked about retirement accounts. And at still another branch they explained that they were relocating to Hong Kong and asked for detailed information about global financial services. Susan hadn't had this much fun in years.

It was dark when Mark and Susan got back to the bank's headquarters. Susan stopped in the ladies' room, and when she rounded the corner back into the office, she saw Mark sitting alone at a table. Stopping for a moment, she watched him through a large potted palm. He had some cards spread out on the table in front of him. Were they the cards he had collected this afternoon? She strained to see. He was writing something on the back of one of them. Picking it up, he read it and smiled softly. Then he scooped up the cards and dropped them into an envelope. Except the one he had written on. That one he carefully placed in his inside jacket pocket, on the left side. He patted it gently with his hand, then slid the envelope containing the rest of the cards into his briefcase. Susan's curiosity soared.

● ● ●

Over the next weeks, everything came together. Susan and Mark worked closely on the presentation to be given to the bank's top management. Their ideas flowed, and more than once they found themselves saying the same words in unison, then stopping and looking at each other and dissolving into laughter. The presentation practically wrote itself—it seemed so effortless, so right.

Then the day arrived. Susan woke early, nervous and excited. *This must be what it's like waking up on your wedding day,* she thought to herself. *Happy and scared at the same time.*

When she arrived, Mark was already in the conference room. She was shocked to see that another early arrival was Ted Pike, the company's CEO. She had met Pike once before, when she first joined the bank; since then she had seen him only at the annual holiday parties. He was unfailingly cordial and had the reputation of being a genuinely nice man, but Susan couldn't help feeling overawed, as though she were in the presence of royalty. Was their project really worth the CEO's time?

*A*lways he kept the card
in the pocket nearest his heart—every day
through all the months he had worked with her.

The moment Pike saw Susan, he got to his feet and extended his hand. "How nice to see you again, Susan." She smiled bravely through his crushing grip. "I understand you've been doing some really outstanding work for us."

"Well, I hope so, Mr. Pike. I guess we're about to find out."

Everyone laughed, and Susan moved to the head of the table. Mark deliberately turned his back to the others and gave Susan a long smile. He placed his right hand gently on his chest—just over his heart, she thought. Something about the gesture made her feel safe.

They made the presentation jointly, first an overview of the bank's history, then an analysis of its current position. Finally, they were ready to present their blueprint for QuantaBank's new branding. As they turned to the crucial slide, Susan realized she was more worried for Mark's sake than for her own. For a moment they both hesitated, locked in one another's gaze—the pause would have seemed barely perceptible to the audience; to the two of them it was lingering, supportive, comforting. Mark's warm gray eyes gave her all the confidence she would ever need.

Then they offered up their branding strategy.

"A strong brand has human characteristics, a definable personality that customers can recognize and relate to. Based on our research, we feel that the following characteristics best define the current strengths of the QuantaBank brand and best position it for the future."

The words glowed on the screen, the product of Susan's work with Mark over the past many weeks:

Honest
Humorous
Forthright
Gentle
Caring

Susan's eyes swept the room for reactions. Some smiled approvingly, others jotted notes on their handouts, still others gazed thoughtfully at the screen, as if absorbing the words. Then someone started applauding, and someone else joined in, until nearly the whole meeting was applauding their efforts. It was not the polite, halfhearted applause that sometimes followed presentations; it was spontaneous and real and heartfelt. For a moment, Susan was overwhelmed with emotion—she didn't know whether to laugh or cry. Another warm look from Mark steadied her.

Greg sat stony-faced, stroking a gold fountain pen on the conference table before him. The muscles of his jaw pulsed under his taut skin. Without looking up at Susan or Mark, he said in a loud voice, "The image you propose isn't corporate. This is not a corporate brand."

Susan had seen that look on Greg's face before: coldly angry, calculating, ready to do anything to destroy his opponent. She would not let him hurt Mark. Her delicate cheeks flushed with scarlet rage.

And yet Mark was calm. "You're right," he said to Greg. "It's not a traditional corporate brand."

"But we're a bank," Greg snarled, raising his hard green eyes in challenge. "Surely you know what a bank is. How is a bank 'gentle' or 'humorous'? I'm afraid your thinking eludes me."

"A bank is a service organization," replied Mark evenly. "An organization of people working for people. It doesn't matter what the interface is—in the branches, on the phone, over the Internet. The bank is a human-based organization. With a human face."

"Our competitors don't have human faces," Greg shot back.

"That's right," said Mark.

"That's *exactly* right," Ted Pike intoned, and faces all around the table turned in his direction. Susan had nearly forgotten that the CEO of the most powerful bank in the world was sitting in the room. Pike dropped his large hand decisively on the conference table: "I think this is the competitive edge we've been trying to find all this time."

Unawed by the man's praise, Mark warmed to the subject. "You know, Mr. Pike, I believe that the very best branding is branding that tells the truth, and I think this position is entirely reflective of the truth of this bank. I've spent a lot of time with your people, and I've visited a bunch of the branches. You have really good people, and this *is* a human organization. This is one of those happy situations where it's the real life and culture of the organization that can drive the branding. You've got something really strong here, and to try to cover it under a cloak of corporate anonymity would be a crime."

Susan loved him. She knew it now. She had loved him from the first moment she saw him, that first day in her office. There was no use trying to deny it. He seemed to know her so well, so much better than any man had before . . .

• • •

The next two months were the busiest of Susan's life. She was put in charge of disseminating the new branding position throughout the bank and embraced the assignment with all her energy and talent. She hired a team of trainers and held meetings in every division. She and Mark worked hand-in-hand, and the weeks flew by. Greg became more distant. Susan hardly noticed.

She lavished all her attention on the project—for her, it was a labor of love. Even once the training team was up to speed, Susan tried to attend as many staff meetings as she could. She was intrigued with the idea of the brand communicating values, and she was gratified at the enthusiastic response from employees.

One evening she stopped in to a training session at the Court Street branch—the one she had visited with Mark. She watched as the trainer presented the brand personality to a quiet, tired group of tellers.

"Honest
Humorous
Forthright
Gentle
Caring"

It had become a mantra, as familiar to Susan as her own name.

Suddenly a strong female voice rang out from the back of the room. "How do you expect us to be all those things when we only get twenty minutes for lunch?" The voice belonged to a heavyset African-American woman.

The trainer laughed.

The woman did not, nor did the rest of the tellers. "It wasn't a joke, it was a question."

Someone inhaled audibly, then a heavy silence descended. The trainer's eyes cast around the room for support.

After an uncomfortable moment passed, the woman continued: "I cannot be humorous and gentle and caring and all those things when I'm working short-handed and half the time I don't even get to *take* lunch. My *manager* doesn't get to take lunch. You know that's not even *legal?* If this is going to be a change, is it really going to *mean* something?" Murmurs of agreement rose up around her.

The trainer looked helplessly at Susan. His train-the-trainer sessions hadn't prepared him for this.

Susan stood up. "The whole point of this branding is that it's supposed to mean something," she said. "It's not just window-dressing. And the situation you describe is *not* consistent with the identity of the bank. I'll look into it. I promise you I will."

Afterwards, Susan took the trainer out for a drink and a pep talk, and then, although it was well after dark, she returned to the office. She sat at her desk, musing about the meeting. Reaching for the phone, she dialed Mark's cellular. It rang once. She abruptly hung up. *Susan,* she said firmly to herself, *you know what to do.* Opening her e-mail program, she addressed a new message:

piket@quantabank.com <Ted Pike, CEO>
Subject: Branding in the Real World

• • •

Two months later, on a rainy evening in early spring, Susan sat among smiling colleagues at a banquet table in Easton's elegant ballroom. The branding project had been a brilliant success, and Ted Pike had written her personally to thank her for alerting him to the problems in the Court Street branch, which had since been resolved by hiring more staff. Greg had requested and received a transfer to the Denver office, and the way seemed clear for Susan to become head of marketing for the entire bank.

Mark's arrival made her happiness complete. He sat down next to her, in a seat that she had strategically piled with her purse and her sweater and a couple of extra programs. The dinner was like a happy dream.

As the dessert arrived, Mark leaned over to whisper to her. His head was close to hers, and she could feel the warmth radiating from him. "Susan, can I talk to you for a moment? I have something to tell you. Can we go somewhere and talk for a minute?" Her heart racing, Susan followed Mark to a quiet area at the back of the ballroom, a small balcony overlooking the sweeping marble staircase that rose up from the elegant lobby.

Mark took her arm and began speaking in his soft, gentle voice. "I wanted to let you know that I've taken a position in our Tokyo office. I'm not sure how much good I'm going to do there, but it'll be a change of scene."

They were both silent for a moment. Susan could hear her heart pounding in her ears. She tried to speak, but she couldn't. One word and one word only revolved in her head: *Why? Why?* she thought desperately. *A change of scene? Why? What about me? What about us?*

"I'm leaving tonight," he said ruefully.

Suddenly everything seemed very far away, unreal. Susan felt her cheeks flush hot and red. The air around her seemed thick and heavy.

"But you can't leave, Mark," she said, her voice small and weak. "We still need you. We need you on the project."

He shook his head. "Susan, you know that's not true. I think the truth is you never really needed me at all. You had all the right ideas—there was nothing here you couldn't have done all on your own."

Susan struggled to reply. Then, through the haze, she became aware of people's eyes on her. Her friends at the table were laughing and waving to her. She heard Ted Pike's strong voice over the microphone, "Well, where can she have gotten to? She's probably gone back to the office to do some more work." Laughter rippled through the room. "Susan, are you out there?"

She realized in horror that Ted was introducing her to the whole company, congratulating her for her achievement. She felt empty. What did that matter now? Not now, not at this moment. She couldn't. She wanted to run, to hide, to fly into Mark's arms. But Mark gently pushed her away.

Pike suddenly spotted her at the back of the room.

"Well, there you are," he said jovially. "I was right—you two are still working! Well, take a little break, Susan, and come up here so we can let you know how much we appreciate everything you've done." Pike stepped back from the podium, inviting her up with a large sweeping gesture.

Susan heard the crowd's good-natured laughter as if it were a distant, muffled sound. She saw herself approaching the podium, picking up the microphone. Nothing was real. It was all a dream. She heard her own voice, small and distant, thanking people for their contributions. She spoke of her feelings about the project—it was like listening to someone else's words. Tears welled up in her eyes, and she fell silent. Her colleagues stood and began applauding. Soon the whole audience was on its feet, beaming approval and filling the ballroom with deafening applause. Through it all, Susan saw only Mark, standing at the back of the room, applauding and gazing at her with what looked like love. It *looked* like love in his eyes. How could she have been so wrong? Blinking back tears, she returned silently to the table.

"Susan, I'm so sorry," Mark said. "My car is waiting. I'm sorry the timing was so awkward. I didn't mean for this to happen. Susan, I have to go now."

"Let me walk you to the door," she said numbly. They moved in silence down the long winding staircase, the only sound their footfalls on the marble. Her heart was racing; her mind was frozen. Together she and Mark walked across the gleaming lobby floor, through the revolving door and out into the rain.

"I've been meaning to give you this," Mark said. He pulled a worn envelope from his trench coat and pressed it into her hand. "Thank you very much, Susan. For everything. I don't know how to thank you. Susan, I don't know what to say." He reached out and gently took her hand. The next moment, he was gone.

• • •

Mark slumped in the back of the taxi. He reached absently into his inner jacket pocket for his airline ticket and passport. Wearily, he checked his itinerary. Refolding the documents, he slid them back into the pocket. And suddenly he sat bolt upright. It wasn't there. Frantically, he began emptying all of his pockets, dumping the contents onto the seat next to him. Then he threw open his briefcase and pawed roughly through the papers. It wasn't there. He pulled everything out, looked through all the folders, turned all of his pockets inside out. And still it wasn't there.

Bedraggled and crying, Susan walked alone into the huge empty lobby. Her dress, its dusty rose silk now soaking with rain, clung sadly to her delicate form. The coat-check girl stared openly at her; two early departers from the party, a man and a woman in evening dress, glanced at her and looked quickly away. Slowly and deliberately, Susan began to climb the long marble staircase. The sounds of the party echoed from the ballroom above. Everyone would see, she thought. But it didn't matter. Nothing mattered. She had lost everything. Without ever really having had it, she had lost it all.

Suddenly, she became aware of the envelope in her hand. From him, it was from him. *Oh please, let it be* . . . She hardly knew what she wished for—all she knew was that she had never wanted anything so much in her life. Eagerly, she tore open the envelope and found inside . . . her own business cards. *He promised he would return them—on that first day.* She smiled weakly; always true to his word. It seemed like a lifetime ago that she had given them to Mark. She had been a different person then. Now she knew she would never be the same, never ever again. Through the blur of her tears, she saw something written on the back of one of them. *Oh God, did I give him cards with other people's numbers on them?* She looked more closely. The handwriting was not hers, it was Mark's. Blinking back the hot tears, she stopped on the stairs and read the words.

"Susan," the card said.

"Susan.
"Susan = honest
Susan = humorous
Susan = forthright
Susan = gentle
Susan = caring"

Her breath caught in her throat. He *did* love her. She hadn't been wrong. Susan turned, flinging away from her all but the one card—the one card that said everything, everything she had ever wanted to hear— and began racing down the long marble staircase, her high-heeled shoes clacking loudly on the marble. She had to find him.

• • •

"Turn around—we've got to go back!" Mark snapped at the driver. Where was it? It was always there. He had kept it there ever since that day with her, the day in the coffee shop, the day he had first known. Al-

$\mathscr{S}$usan turned, flinging away from her all but the one card, the one card that said everything, everything she had ever wanted to hear ...

ways he kept the card in the pocket nearest his heart—every day through all the months he had worked with her. And now he couldn't leave without it. Losing her was enough, too much, unbearable. To lose this token as well was unimaginably cruel.

The driver grumbled and made a U-turn at the next light. The rain began to fall harder.

Susan burst through the door and out into the rain. *A cab,* she thought, *it will be a miracle to find a cab in this weather. But I have to, I have to find him. I can't let him go. If it takes a miracle, then that's what I have to have.*

The rain came in torrents now. It beat savagely on Susan's head and shoulders. It swelled the small rivulet in the gutter to a dangerous current. It clattered on the sidewalk like gunfire.

And out of the blinding storm Susan saw the lights of a taxi approaching. He was pulling over, pulling up in front of the building where Susan stood. Heedless of the small river that now coursed through the gutter, Susan ran over to the car.

Its door began to open. Reaching for the handle, Susan lost her grip on the card—Mark's card, the only trace she had left of him. It fell to the pavement and landed in a little swirl of rain on the sidewalk, and the ink immediately began to run. *Lost, lost,* she thought, *all I'll ever have of him, and it's lost.* She reached for it. At the same time a hand reached for it from the back of the open cab. The hands touched. Susan looked up. It was Mark.

"Susan," he said, his voice racked with pain. He gripped her arm and drew her to him, crushing her against his powerful chest. Susan's head fell back, her golden curls clinging to her filmy silk dress, her mouth eagerly seeking his. They kissed, a tempest more powerful than the heavens could ever have imagined—the driving rain around them seemed a gentle shower by comparison. Time stood still, and there was no one but them in the entire universe.

Mark's eyes filled with tears. "Oh Susan," he breathed desperately, "Susan! Forgive me. I didn't want to hold you back. I wasn't sure how you felt. Susan, I've never loved anyone the way I love you. If only you knew how much I love you—if only I could tell you."

"You already have," she said, smiling gently and holding up the wet business card. Traces of his writing still remained, traces of the words he

*S*usan reached for it. At the same time
a hand reached for it from the back of the open cab.
The hands touched.

had written about her. "You already have, Mark. I understand." And the two again fell into a deep, passionate kiss—a kiss that would never end for the rest of their lives.

WHAT DOES THE BUSINESS PARABLE MEAN?

Well, this parable wasn't particularly subtle, was it? But we hope it made you laugh, and perhaps cry, nonetheless. The story does focus on some important issues about branding. Many of these are made explicit by our hero and heroine. But the most important of them bear repeating.

Unfortunately, most branding is not organic to the company itself. Think about your own bank, for example. Can you remember how it brands itself? Now think about how your bank's biggest rival brands itself. Does the word *interchangeable* come to mind? We think this is a problem. And it's a problem not limited to banks.

A company's branding should be intimately related to its organizational values and practices. This is why Susan and Mark visit the bank branches, and it's why Susan attends the on-site training sessions. It's also why Susan takes the risk of contacting her CEO when she finds a serious problem in one of the branches. At this point in the story, Greg—the voice of traditional, conservative marketing—washes his hands of her. To him, branding belongs in the marketing department and nowhere else. But Susan's notion of the brand promise is that everybody in the organization should be involved.

In addition, there is the recurring theme of knowledge and self-knowledge in the story. Susan observes that Greg has never made the effort to get to know her. She falls in love with Mark because he does. And it is Mark's knowledge of Susan that enables him to make the leap of faith and brand the entire organization based mainly on her character. Our point here is that intimate knowledge of an organization is important to good branding. If branding is related only to the external—if it's just pasted on from the outside and used only for external image projection—then companies need to have the honesty to face themselves and know themselves. If they find things they don't like, they need to have the courage to change those things. That's the job of the Branding Mastercraft in The Garage.

IS EVERYTHING A BRAND?

The concept of branding has drastically changed over the last decade. "I understand that CINDY CRAWFORD is a brand," says supermodel Cindy Crawford. "When I hire someone, as assistants or whatever, I always say, 'Look, we all work for CINDY CRAWFORD—myself included.' "[15] Cindy Crawford's comment in the January 2000 issue of *Vogue* magazine tells us that brands are no longer understood just as the brand marks—the logos and labels—that we used to apply to cattle, container ships, industrial packages, and canned consumer products in the supermarket. The concept of branding has been gradually broadened into many other forms of commercial—and even noncommercial—offers. In fact, Crawford's remark also lets us know that everything is now viewed as a brand, not just the cereal boxes in the supermarkets and the clothes in the designer boutiques. As a result, any organization or individual needs to be concerned with branding.

The key principles of branding apply equally to produce, places, and people. Logos and imagery are found on bananas, vine-ripened tomatoes, and English cucumbers. Cities and countries like Singapore and Britain have hired brand experts to revamp their image. And in one of his latest books, Tom Peters, management ur-guru and self-declared brand fanatic, has offered fifty ideas for "Brand Me." In this new brand-crazy world, commodities—and "real" people—exist only until some clever marketing manager (or PR manager, or image consultant) decides to brand them.

Another change is that brands are considered extremely valuable in and of themselves. Interbrand, a global branding agency, has estimated the value of Coca-Cola, the most valuable brand in the world, to constitute over 95 percent of all the company's corporate assets.[16] To be sure, brand value depends on the nature of the product category and industry: it is higher for luxury goods than for utilities, for instance. Yet Interbrand also found that brand value is growing in practically every single industry.

BRANDING IN THE GARAGE

In The Garage, branding techniques can be found everywhere. Of course, products are branded, but so are the promotional campaigns related to

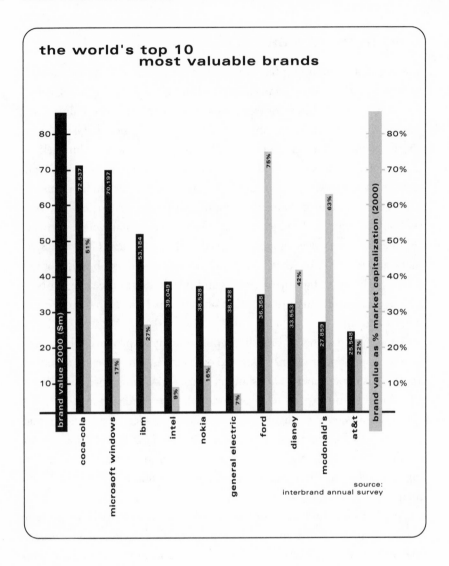

the world's top 10
most valuable brands

brand value 2000 ($m)

brand value as % market capitalization (2000)

coca-cola 72,537 51%

microsoft windows 70,197 17%

ibm 53,184 27%

intel 39,049 9%

nokia 38,528 16%

general electric 38,128 7%

ford 36,368 75%

disney 33,553 42%

mcdonald's 27,859 63%

at&t 25,548 22%

source:
interbrand annual survey

these products, and so in fact is the corporation as a whole, its divisions and its projects.

Indeed, many companies that have traditionally focused on the branding of their individual products have discovered the corporate brand as a key new marketing initiative. Think, for example, about the formerly faceless companies in the pharmaceutical industries that have recently emerged with branded personalities. Because branding can apply to an entire organization, then, everybody in the organization has a role to play in managing the brand. To represent the brand in the right way, all employees need to know the brand and live it. In a wide variety of situations—when meeting customers, when communicating to the public, and at trade shows and conferences—employees are representing the corporate brand and should be prepared to engage in behavior that is consistent with it. The disgruntled bank teller in the business parable above understands firsthand that branding should be more than just a collection of slogans, and she protests when reality doesn't align with the bank's brand identity. Increasingly, employees and customers alike expect branding to reflect the truth about a company and its offerings.

As we will see throughout this chapter, this idea can become the anchor point of an entirely new way of looking at an organization. It can become the center point of all the branding and reputation efforts of The Garage. And it is—paradoxically—much more tangible and livable and value-adding than all the corporate mumbo jumbo of "mission," "values," and "core competencies," because branding—if done right—marries the outside and the inside: communication and action.

However, this "marriage" requires that we view branding as a Mastercraft. The mastercraft approach blends *bizz, buzz,* and *stuff* in branding initiatives. Good branding needs *the buzz* to differentiate the corporation from others. Good branding also needs *the stuff,* the products and services that make the corporation shine. Finally, good branding requires a strategic approach. Branding does not just "happen"; great branding is the result of leadership, strategy, and planning—good branding needs *the bizz.* We must embrace the notion of a brand as a directional and unifying force within the organization that allows anyone in the organization to use the brand to guide their decisions. The brand is thus an ideal tool for organizational alignment and for infusing creativity into organizational projects.

MASTERCRAFTING THE BRAND: THE FIVE STEPS

There are five steps in mastercrafting the brand. Let us discuss each in turn.

brandCORE

The brandCORE of AOL is "community." The brandCORE of Virgin is that of an innovative, underdog, fun service company. The brandCORE of Jaguar is "elegance."

The brandCORE is not a logo, an advertising slogan, or a tagline. However, a definite understanding of brandCORE is critical for creating the right taglines and ad slogans. The brandCORE is not an empty positioning or mission statement sitting on a piece of paper or hanging on the wall. The brandCORE, as brand strategist Chris Macrae has called it, is the "living script of the organization."

The brandCORE exists not only for image projection; once an organization understands its brandCORE, its employees and the entire organization will live it. It does not even have to be verbalized—it is understood. It has become the grammar of the organization; the metaphor it lives by. It must be felt by any customer or visitor who comes in contact with the organization, its products, and its people. That's why Disney employees are "actors" and why Disney buildings are cartoon castles. That's why Gap employees wear casual clothing and why the W Hotels check-in people wear black.

Do you know the brandCORE of your organization?

Searching for a brandCORE requires a lot from an organization and its management—along the lines of what Susan and Mark go through in our business parable. It requires, first and foremost, a consideration of core values. However, not in the sense of coming up with vague generalities that result in inward-looking backpatting. The brandCORE needs to be communicated—in a straightforward, believable, and catchy way. So, that eliminates any complicated strategy statement (because it is not straightforward); any sort of "competence," "adding value to all customers and suppliers," "best quality" terminology (because it is not believable); and any overtechnical industry jargon (because it is not catchy).

Moreover, brandCORE should express the dynamic business concept of the organization which creates the organization's competitive advantage. The competitive advantage may exist at various levels of generality. At the highest level, it may consist of operational efficiency, superb service, quality sourcing, outstanding added value, or fast scalability. At a

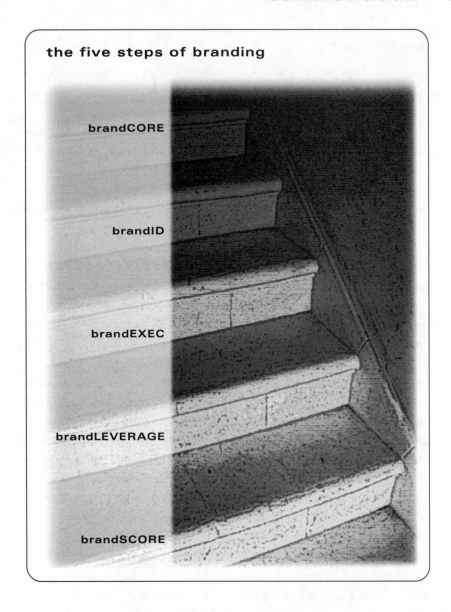

the five steps of branding

brandCORE

brandID

brandEXEC

brandLEVERAGE

brandSCORE

more specific level, it may consist of the special way in which operational efficiency is executed, for example, in terms of speed, or availability around the clock, or geographic reach; or the specific way in which service is provided, for example, in the sense of high, personal touch; a great integration of click and mortar; customized service delivery; and so on.

brandID

Once an organization has a clear understanding of its brandCORE, it needs to move on to the second step of mastercrafting its brand: the organization needs to create a brandID in line with its brandCORE.

The brandID entails the naming system related to the brand. What do we call the products and the various initiatives and programs on a global scale?

The brandID also entails the key visual identity of the corporate brand and its various product brands. What are our signature colors? What typefaces do we use? What tone of voice do we use when we greet customers, when we service them, when we interact with each other?

Finally, the brandID entails the brand architecture. How many levels of brand architecture should we create? Should we have a corporate brand, divisional subbrands, master brands, subbrands, product brands, and models? Or fewer levels? Should we have one corporate master brand and/or endorsement brands? Should we have stand-alone brands?

Starting in the nineties, the trend has been to create sophisticated brand architectures. The "pure" approaches of a monolithic branding (the classic Sony approach) or a stand-alone branding (the classic Procter & Gamble approach) have given way to more complex and malleable approaches in which part of the company's offerings may be labeled by the corporate name; others may be endorsed by the corporate name; and still others may be stand-alone brands. Consider Sony. There are still lots of Sony branded products. But then there is the Sony Walkman and Sony Playstation, which are becoming brands on their own and which at some point in time may become stand-alone brands.

The decision about which approach to use for a specific product can be facilitated by the use of a decision tree that lists various business and industry criteria. The key issues include an examination of a company's existing brand architecture, where it would ideally like to go, and within that context asking two questions: "What can this product do for the company?" and "What can this company do for this product?" We can then label it appropriately.

Once again, it is important to stress that brandID, like branding in general, is not only for image projection. It is also an anchor point, a natural way of talking, communicating, and organizing the various things that an organization does. If the organization decides that a brand is a stand-alone, then its structures and expectations should change accordingly. Branding decisions are not isolated decisions delegated down to a marketing department.

brandEXEC

brandEXEC, the next step in mastercrafting the brand, concerns the execution of the brandCORE and brandID. brandEXEC includes a clear understanding of what we could call the "executional masterbrief." This masterbrief specifies the type of core messages, the type of core symbols, and the type of core communication and behavioral approach that the organization creates for the brand's customers. It may include what type of environment the organization will create for its employees or, in the form of a city plaza, for the public at large.

brandEXEC is not pure image projection. brandEXEC also occurs every day in the corporate dining room, in the type of dress people wear (including on "casual Friday"), in the language that employees use, in the medium (e.g., phone, e-mail, fax) they use to respond to customers.

brandLEVERAGE

Step four, brandLEVERAGE, ranges from straightforward line extension to broad-based brand extension decisions. It also concerns co-branding efforts and expansions into new media or new markets.

Over the last few years, the topic of brand extensions has attracted a lot of research. What do customers think when a car manufacturer licenses its name to sunglasses? What if it is Porsche? What if it is Volkswagen? How about if it is the Volkswagen Beetle? It turns out that the perceptions depend on whether there is a fit—in terms of features, concepts, lifestyles, or technologies—between the two products. It depends on the brand image (Porsche can pull it off; so can the Beetle; but the overall image of Volkswagen, a "people's car," isn't quite trendy enough). Then there is the backfire effect: a brand extension that fails and undermines established equity.

The studies have been focused, however, almost exclusively on the "image projection" function of brandLEVERAGE. Yet brandLEVERGE also has an internal dimension: in manufacturing and strategic decision making. There are issues of production runs or outsourcing; and of where the organization wants to go and how this affects the customer's perceptions of core products.

brandSCORE

The final step in mastercrafting the brand is brandSCORE. We use the term to refer to a tracking and measurement system of the market that can be used for brand planning, personnel monitoring, and strategic decision making. The brandSCORE system is typically established at three levels of generality: at the level of "media effectiveness"; at the level of "brand equity"; and in terms of the financial value of the firm.

What is missing, however, in all the excitement about measuring media effectiveness, brand equity, and brand valuations, is actually the key information for managing brands. The key question is: How do I build which aspect of brand equity through which medium so that I enhance the overall value of the brand? This issue concerns the connection and relation between the three levels, not accuracy, reliability, and methodological sophistication at each level. Ideally, that model needs to be built on an individual industry, or even firm, basis. Whether to use the Web or print or the radio (a medium) to arouse attention (an aspect of brand equity) to affect Wall Street (brand valuation) depends a great deal on who does it. With enough data and a systematic approach, it is possible to build such three-tier models—and once they are built, they facilitate market decisions as well as internal decisions (e.g., in terms of the workstyles and relations with communications agencies; in terms of who launches and how new products are being launched; in terms of who is accountable for the health of a brand).

ORGANIZATIONAL ALIGNMENT AROUND THE BRAND PROMISE

As we have illustrated, organizational alignment around the brand promise is the key imperative in The Garage. Organizational alignment is concerned with the values and behaviors of employees when they are interacting with organizational constituents and thus representing the brand.[17]

Personnel alignment is the most critical issue. Everyone in the organization needs to "live" the brand. This does not mean just following the

unmasking the brand

guidelines developed by the internal "brand police" in terms of its identity manuals. It includes the voice and behavior used by every employee whenever he or she represents the organizational brand. Sounds like Big Brother of the branding variety? Actually, it is more like unmasking the brand, that is, using the brand not just as an external projection device but for expressing corporate reality. Therefore, the brandCORE needs to be developed with knowledge of the organizational culture and employee personality.

Alignment can be an immense challenge for an organization. Let's look at three examples that illustrate how tricky this can be.

In 2000, Eli Lilly, the pharmaceutical firm, launched a new brand initiative around the brandline "Answers that matter." The brand slogan appeared on all the business cards, on a revamped, more customer-friendly Web site, and was about to be launched on all product communications. The idea was to provide vital answers to all the constituents of the organization—doctors, hospitals, HMOs, the government, and of course the pa-

Brand Protest Against Image Projection

For the first time in three decades, the youth movement is back. And unlike its predecessor in the 1960s, today's youth movement is not a protest movement. The movement is essentially commercial. It is an enthusiastic embrace of capitalism; the motivation for techno geeks and MBA students is the same: get rich quick.

But don't be fooled, argues Naomi Klein, a Canadian journalist whose work has appeared in the *Toronto Globe & Mail, The Village Voice,* and *The Battler.* According to Ms. Klein, underneath all that excitement there is another revolution brewing—a revolution more in tune with the 1960s than the early 2000s.

In her book *No Logo: Taking Aim at the Brand Bullies,* and in various magazine interviews, Klein has argued that scaled-up logos not only appear on every product we see but are also polluting our environment by turning up nearly everywhere else, including in schools and universities. In this totally branded world, not even public spaces are left unbranded, thus changing our cityscapes drastically. The visible result of this mass branding, according to Klein, is "no choice" and "teen clones" who all dress the same.

> The Kinko's Starbucks and Blockbuster clerks buy their uniform of Khakis and white and blue shirts at the Gap; the "Hi! Welcome to the Gap!" greeting cheer is fueled by Starbucks double espressos; the resumes that got them the jobs were designed at Kinko's on friendly Mac's, in 12-point Helvetica on Microsoft Word. The troops show up for work smelling of CK One (except at Starbucks, where colognes and perfumes are thought to compete with the "romance of coffee" aroma), their faces freshly scrubbed with Body Shop Blue Corn Mask, before leaving apartments furnished with Ikea self-assembled bookcases and coffee tables.[18]

Moreover, the decision to concentrate on marketing and branding rather than manufacturing has led to a cheap outsourced and subcontracted production process that grossly underpays workers in emerging markets, causing levels of exploitation similar to the nineteenth century. For example, whereas a garment worker in the United States earns an average of U.S.$10 an hour, Chinese workers in special economic zones work under appalling and unsafe conditions for as little as 13 cents an hour, a fraction of the 87 cents estimated by labor groups to be a living wage.

Now a protest movement has arisen to address these issues. Klein maintains that the protest movement is showing up in a variety of ways: "culture jamming" (the practice of parodying ads and billboards to alter the message at public spaces); "reclaiming the streets" (anti-brand street demonstrations in the UK); shareholder resolutions against, for example, sweatshop practices; and student protests.

Similar initiatives include complaint Web sites such as eComplaints.com, epinions.com or feedbackdirect.com, and all sorts of "sucks" Web sites that organize public concerns and allow consumers to express their opinions, make suggestions, and post their complaints online. Since the complaints are neatly sorted into categories we all recognize from the main search engines, these sites allow consumers to convey their concerns easily to a broad audience. As one such site declares on its home page: "eComplaints is your chance to fight back. It's your chance to be heard by the company at fault and more importantly, by your fellow consumer." Thus, private service issues between a company and its customer become public relations and hence brand and reputation management issues.

tients. Clearly, it is an interesting and appropriate brand positioning. But whether or not Lilly can deliver on this promise depends on whether it can provide the right answers in the right time frame to the right constituent in the right medium. That's an enormous challenge and a risky one as well: If Lilly provides the wrong answers as a pharmaceutical firm, it may risk others' lives and end up in court. On the other hand, just using the slogan but not delivering on its promise amounts to an empty promise: if you are lucky, nobody cares; but in the worst case it can result in customer dissatisfaction and perceptions of deceit. So, the new brand slogan offers the opportunity to align the organization around the brand promise, and if it is done well, it differentiates Lilly in the marketplace in a powerful way. It may even speed up the efficiency and accuracy with which Lilly employees provide answers to each other. As this book goes to press, Eli Lilly works on this challenge.

Here is another example, this time from the insurance industry. Clarica, formerly the Mutual Life Insurance Company of Canada, adopted its new name in 1999 and embarked on a brand alignment initiative in 2000. The goals of the initiative were speaking with clarity and delivering the personality attributes of being approachable, full of vitality, knowledgeable, and straightforward. Once again, the issue was how to align the organization around the brand promise. In this case, the challenge included understanding of what clarity means in a certain context, how it can be measured, and how employees (in particular, the insurance agents) can be given incentives to deliver clarity.

Finally, the issue of alignment arises especially in a global context. Whether you are a global consumer-packaged-goods firm, a cosmetics firm, or a nonprofit organization, you need to make sure that the brand is understood and internalized similarly around the world. Not everything around the world has to be identical (the ad campaigns may need to be localized; the packaging perhaps; maybe even the product formula and the ingredients), but the brandCORE promise and positioning, most of the time, should be the same. And this requires organizational alignment on a global scale.

SUMMARY

Branding has changed. It is no longer associated just with logos and signage. Instead, many projects and initiatives may be examined through the lens of branding. Thus, anything an organization does contributes to its brand equity and reputation. As a result, The Garage must make the mastercrafting of its brands (the corporate brand and product brands) a key priority. This requires that we manage the five steps of mastercrafting brands and that we align the organization around the brand promise.

In the next chapter, we turn to mastercrafting the customer experience. As we will see, the creative organization brings *bizz, buzz,* and *stuff* to the management of its interaction with customers. Managing the customer experience includes anything from the service interface to experiential communications to customer lifespan management, and more.

the mastercraft of customer experience management

Companies are looking for various ways to form and sustain ongoing relationships with their customers. Companies therefore need to focus on the entire customer experience, and treat *customer experience management (CEM)* as a mastercraft. The following business parable explores one key aspect of CEM, the service experience, from the point of view of the customer—an air traveler on the way to Japan.

"The Haiku on Board"

"Flight SQ 011
from LA to Tokyo
now ready to board"

Robert moved slowly down the jetway. He had missed the first-class preboarding and was now shuffling along with the rest of the passengers on the Tokyo-bound Singapore Airlines flight. Two men walked ahead of

A flight attendant,
her thick black hair shining in the soft light,
greeted him by name.

him. One wore a dark blue business suit, striped tie, crisp white shirt, and gold cufflinks; he carried a black leather briefcase. He looked more like he was going into an important meeting than boarding an overnight flight. *I'll bet he turns right,* thought Robert, *into business class.* The other guy was wearing jeans and sneakers. He carried a backpack over one shoulder. First class? Robert liked this guessing game, and he was usually right.

It was hot at the end of the jetway, the air off the blazing tarmac slipping through the accordion seal, carrying with it fumes from jet fuel and who knew what else from L.A.'s July air.

It was a relief to step onto the plane. Suddenly it was cool, hushed, slightly dark. The air conditioning created a soft breeze. A flight attendant, her thick black hair shining in the soft light, greeted him by name. She wore the Singapore Airlines uniform, a colorful batik print dress that draped her body closely. He had read something about these uniforms—they had been made by a French designer, based on the traditional Malaysian sarong.

Turning to his left, Robert followed the flight attendant forward, passing Jeans & Sneakers, who was settling into his seat in the rear of the first-class cabin, pulling a sleek laptop out of his pack. He was right about that one, Robert thought. Probably some kind of Internet start-up type.

The flight attendant's uniform fit a bit tight, hugging the curve of her hip. She turned swiftly and with a fluid motion of her hand indicated his seat. He quickly looked up to her face, but it was too late—he had been caught staring.

Robert had requested the seat in the very front of the cabin. The seats in first class were arranged in a kind of pyramid shape, with a single seat at the very front. *Like a flock of geese,* Robert thought, *or fighter jets in formation.* Not everyone liked this front seat—some found it too isolated, others felt it claustrophobic. But to Robert, it evoked potency: to sit at the front of the plane, beneath the flight deck and actually well in front of it, literally at the very tip of the airframe. In this seat, he arrived just slightly before everyone else—including the pilot.

It was really more like a small room than an airplane seat—they called it a "sky suite." The seat itself was upholstered in Connoly Leather, like a Jaguar MKII, soft and mildly fragrant. It was a wing-chair design, giving

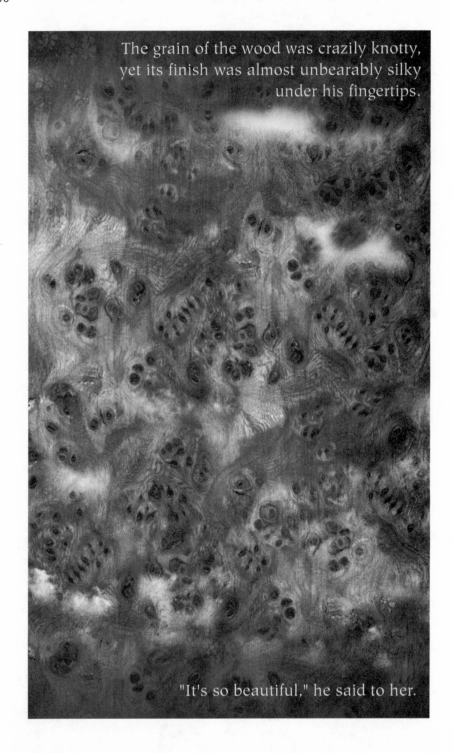

The grain of the wood was crazily knotty, yet its finish was almost unbearably silky under his fingertips.

"It's so beautiful," he said to her.

the passenger a quiet and private environment. The entire suite was framed with rich, warm burlwood. The flight attendant gently placed one hand on the tabletop facing the seat; with the other, she made a welcoming gesture. Robert noticed her hands were small, with slim tapering fingers. He ran his hand along the smooth, cool surface of the wood. The grain of the wood was crazily knotty, yet its finish was almost unbearably silky under his fingertips. "It's so beautiful," he said to her.

She smiled. "There is a layer of fiberglass on top of the wood," she replied softly. "To protect it and make it more beautiful." She formed the words carefully and deliberately. It made Robert wonder what she was really thinking as she spoke.

"May I take your jacket for you, sir?" she asked. He handed it to her, to be carefully placed on a hanger and tucked in some safe place. At the end of the flight, long after he had forgotten the jacket, she would bring it again to him. *Almost like a gift, a surprise.* She asked him when he would like to be served dinner. "No dinner," he said. "Just caviar. Give me about two and a half hours. I need to get through some reading." "Of course, sir. Can I bring you anything in the meantime?" "Just some water would be great," he replied. "Thanks." The flight attendant disappeared with the jacket, as Robert set about moving into his suite. She returned silently with a cold bottle of Evian and a glass chilled to the perfect temperature.

Robert leaned back, aware of the sounds of activity behind him—solid doors locking snugly, fasteners snapped into place. He watched the pre-takeoff safety video on the individual screen in front of his seat. He had seen the video so many times he felt he knew the actress who did the narration, yet he always watched it carefully, as if for the first time. He listened intently to the Japanese, entirely unable to understand it yet somehow finding comfort in the oddly familiar words. He remembered visiting the Catholic cathedral in Shanghai and hearing a group of very old people saying the rosary in Chinese. He imagined the passengers in business class, reading the *Wall Street Journal* and entirely ignoring the video. He thought of the man in the blue business suit.

The plane taxied to the runway. It felt bumpy today, in a hurry, perhaps. His seat in the nose of the plane restricted his view—there were no windows nearby. It meant he had to experience the flight entirely by sensation and sound, not sight. A brief pause, and then the tight hairpin turn.

He knew they were at the top of the runway. Another brief pause, almost ritualistic, and then the aircraft accelerated. The four wing-mounted engines generated tremendous velocity in a matter of seconds. He enjoyed the feeling of being pushed back into his seat—he almost wished for even greater force.

As they took off, Robert's location in the nose of the plane gave him a sensation he never felt anywhere else: the slight sense of hesitation as the aircraft left the ground, almost like brakes being applied, although he knew that was impossible. He leaned back in the leather seat and closed his eyes. It was interesting to him how many people he had seen doing this, as if they were falling asleep. Did people actually sleep during take-off, or was it fear? Or prayer? For Robert, it was a kind of meditation. The ascent was steep. He imagined the blue Pacific glittering beneath them. He felt free.

"Ladies and gentlemen, welcome aboard Singapore Airlines. I am Eva, your purser on the flight today. Our flying time to Tokyo will be approximately ten hours and twenty minutes. We will be starting our beverage service in a few minutes, to be followed shortly by dinner. We hope that you will have a pleasant flight, and please do not hesitate to tell us if there is anything we can do to make your flight more enjoyable."

After the plane had leveled off, Robert got up, stretched, and went into the bathroom to change into the pajamas the airline had supplied for him. Jeans & Sneakers worked furiously on his laptop. He returned to his seat and settled back comfortably into his nook, suddenly recalling one of the airline's former slogans: "The journey is the destination." It was true. *Now more than ever,* he thought—this was their new slogan, he remembered.

He was on his way to Japan again. He had been doing a lot of these international runs over the past two years, and he always asked his assistant to assemble some cultural materials for him to peruse on the way. He looked forward to reading his "culture-ed cookies," as he liked to call them. Meg always found him interesting stuff; he suspected she probably enjoyed finding the material as much as he enjoyed reading it. When he went to Mumbai—as the airlines, but not the Indian businessmen, called it now—she had given him information on meditation techniques. For Beijing, it had been Chinese medicine—essence, energy, spirit: *jing, qi, shen.* And for his last trip to Tokyo, she had prepared a packet about the Japanese bathing tradition—an extended existential experience that contrasted with the typical American quick, perfunctory shower. Meg was kind of a nut, a writer with an Edward Gorey tattoo on her long slim ankle. But the materials she gave him often helped him do business better— he wasn't sure why. He wondered what she had packaged for him this time.

It was part of his ritual to save this culture-ed cookie as a reward for getting through his other in-flight reading—a kind of dessert. Before each flight, he always hit the airport bookstore and bought one business title and one pop-psych book. Once on board, he first browsed some business magazines, then went on to the books. This time the business book turned out to be very heavy going—B2B strategy, abstract and taxing, much harder than it needed to be. *Jeans & Sneakers wouldn't give this stuff a second glance.* He closed it. One down. The pop-psych book was about dealing with stress. You're only stressed if you think you are. Ten attitude adjusters to bust stress. Enough of that.

Good. Finished. Done. Robert delighted in this game of casting off the reading materials. His reward was noticeably lighter luggage when he got off the plane. And of course the culture-ed cookie.

"Would you like more water, sir, or would you like to try our champagne?" The flight attendant had reappeared over his left shoulder. "Just more water for now," he replied. "Could you bring the champagne in about an hour?" "Certainly, sir. Today we can offer you Dom-Pérignon or La Grande Dame. Which would you prefer to have?" La Grande Dame was his favorite champagne. He smiled to himself. *Some choice—the monk or the widow.* It was no contest. "La Grande Dame, please," he said. "Certainly, sir," she replied, "I will bring it in one hour."

In one smooth movement, she produced another bottle of Evian and a fresh glass. For a moment, before she cleared away the empty one, the two bottles stood side by side, reminding him of an Evian ad he had recently seen in a magazine. A beautiful young girl hung over the edge of a white clawfoot bathtub. On the white tiles of the bathroom floor stood a small forest of half-empty Evian bottles, maybe twenty in all. With downcast eyes and wet hair, the girl drapes a long, slim arm over the edge of the tub, her hand perhaps just grazing one of the bottles. Because of the quality of light and focus of the photograph, it was impossible to tell if she was really touching the bottle or not.

He had done that once. Except with champagne. He had been in a hotel in Paris and had ordered ten bottles of champagne for a party in his suite. His guests, a collection of American accountants and insurance lawyers, hadn't touched it. He was left with ten unopened bottles of champagne, plus one given to him by the hotel. He had tried to return them to the catering service, but they had refused. He was flying back to the States the next morning. How could he carry eleven bottles of champagne? It was ridiculous. So he had opened them and poured them into the bath. Popping them open one by one. He opened the window, with its rooftop view of the city. All that was missing was the roses, he thought. He could still remember the sensation of the bubbles on his skin. It had almost been too much.

Two hours into the flight. Time for his cookie. He reached for the materials Meg had prepared for him—this time in a sleek red folder. For the Japanese flag? She always did things like that.

He opened the folder. Inside, it was black and shiny, like a lacquer box. Yes. He smiled.

Under a sheet of fine rice paper, he found a neatly presented set of Internet printouts about the Japanese poetic form, haiku. Still in read-and-discard mode, he first browsed the key points as if it were a business document. Speed-reading lessons had taught him to look for the main ideas, skim the rest, skip what looked unimportant. He wished there were an executive summary. The technique helped him get through piles of paperwork; but this was to be savored. It always took him a little while to unwind. *Relax,* he told himself.

He breathed in slowly through his nose—he remembered that from his Indian meditation—and started reading. "Haiku is a small poem with oriental metric that appeared in the sixteenth century." The printout offered an example by Matsuo Basho:

Old pond
A frog leaps in
Water's sound.

It felt oddly familiar to Robert. Just three lines. It was interesting.

It made him think of Amanpuri, a luxury hotel chain in Southeast

Asia that incorporated elements of indigenous cultures and traditions of the countries in which they were located. He had stayed in this hotel in Phuket that purported to reproduce the old style of Thai life. It was natural, sensual—the antithesis of a business hotel, really. He loved it, the elegance, the slow pace, the protection of luxury. But had the Thais ever really lived this way? Not with fax machines and e-mail and mobile phones. It was an artificial paradise, nostalgia for something that had never been. *Never mind. Relax.*

He had gone out for a walk after one of the violent late afternoon rainstorms that hit every day in Thailand. The sun came out, and it was hot again—hot and wet and close. The sudden downpour had pushed the small pond over the edges of its banks. A little frog looked at him. Its skin looked wet. Had it been drenched, or did its skin look wet all the time? Was it dry to the touch? Was it soft?

His next stop on the trip had been Singapore. He had checked into the hotel, dropped his carry-on bag on the bed, and was firing up his laptop when he thought he saw the bag move. Was it jet lag? he wondered—sometimes it gets worse before it gets better. No, there was something moving in his bag. What the hell was it? He put his hand on it and felt the form through the canvas. It moved. He pushed gently, and it pushed back. Something living. He had a vivid vision of a rabid rat springing from the suitcase and attacking him.

He had called the front desk, and an attendant came up to the room. She looked cautiously at the bag. "Don't worry, sir," she assured him. "We will open your bag downstairs and then return it to you." She had carried the bag away with her, holding it lightly with her long fingers, extended at an unnatural distance from her body. About fifteen minutes later, she reappeared with the bag. She was smiling. "It was a frog in your bag sir," she said. "We set it free in the garden. Here is your bag. Please let us know if you would like to have any of your clothes cleaned, and we will do it for you right away."

For days after that, Robert thought about the frog, unable to shake the idea that the frog in the bag had been the same frog he had seen at Amanpuri. It was absurd, he knew; there was no way it could have gotten into his bag. But had the frog in Amanpuri jumped out of some other traveler's bag?

He returned to his reading. One sentence in the printout caught his attention: "Haiku is done to transcend the limitations imposed by the usual language and the linear/scientific thinking that treats nature and the human being as a machine."

People and machines. During the years he had spent as a manufacturing manager, he found that his most creative engineers were not just engineers—they were incredibly diverse thinkers. Like Einstein. Or Niels Bohr. "The opposite of a correct statement is a false statement, but the opposite of a profound truth may well be another profound truth." He remembered the quotation from a business book he had read on a previous flight. He also remembered that the author had misspelled Bohr's first name. Window-dressing. Mediocre people quoting great thinkers as props for their own mediocrity. He had once somehow been placed on a mailing list for a catalogue of inspirational office products. Page after page of posters, plaques, mugs, pens, key rings, mouse pads—with exhortations like "Achieve," "Innovate," "Imagine." His favorite was a photo of an eagle, with the caption "Soar": funny and grim at the same time. Imagine having to look at that thing all day.

He returned to his reading. The remainder of the document had hyperlinks to *renga* and *renku,* other poetry forms, some cultlike haiku contest in Brazil, a bibliography. His assistant hadn't printed those. He moved on through the packet. He stopped and gazed at a Japanese character that stood for Basho, identified as the greatest haiku poet ever.

"May I serve your champagne now, sir?" La Grande Dame had arrived. He looked at her name tag. "Angela Ng." He wondered how to pronounce it. He wondered what her real name was. Not Angela. With her small, trim hands, she spread a white linen cloth on the burlwood desk and—as if it were part of a ritual—placed the sparkling glass before him. Leaning toward him almost imperceptibly, she remarked on his reading material. "Ah, Basho," she said simply. "Do you read Japanese, sir?" "No, no, I don't," he replied, a bit flustered. He wished he did. Recovering himself, he made an attempt at flirting. "Do you think I'm meeting Mr. Basho in Tokyo?" She smiled and said nothing, then disappeared silently.

He turned to another pile of printouts, www.badhaiku.com. "ABOUT HAIKU" it said in big letters. "Horrible poetry, one line at a time." "Haiku, as far as we can tell, is some sort of Japanese poetry." The usual

With her small, trim hands,
she spread a white linen cloth on the burlwood desk
and, as if it were part of a ritual,
placed the sparkling glass before him.

cool Internet chat. "There is really only one rule. All haiku has 17 syllables structured in a 5/7/5 form."

So basically, if (so ba si caly if)
You can speak in syllables (u can speak in syl la bles)
You can write haiku. (u can write hai ku)

He counted the syllables. He understood the numbers, and found comfort in the formula. A relic of his engineering days. He browsed through a few others.

This is a haiku
Test to see if the new site
Is working. Is it?

Bad01
Bad02
Bad03

This one violated the rules, he noticed. It was not seventeen syllables. It was not arranged 5-7-5. It was also boring. He turned to another printout:

"Does nature—including human nature—speak to you poetically? Learn here how to capture your special moments in nature by recording them in short, evocative poems the Japanese call haiku."

A how-to. Good, he could learn all the rules.

The Web site described a "haiku moment"—a moment of spontaneous inspiration in which the poem happens. It described lying on the grass one summer evening. A firefly comes flying over and, for just a second, you see it set against the constellation Cassiopeia. "In that one brief moment, the firefly has aligned you, the earth, and the universe, and you are reminded that all things are interrelated."

The moment yielded a poem:

stargazing . . .
a firefly joins
Cassiopeia

It was beautiful. The printout went on to explain: "The haiku way is just to say it—simply. Written in a very direct manner, haiku tell the who, what, where, and when of the moment as the author perceived it through his or her senses. The end result of such a concrete description is that the reader feels as if he or she also is having the experience. And because commentary is kept to a minimum, the reader is free to come to his or her own conclusions about what the experience means."

Cool, beautiful. The essence of something; say it simply. Let it be. It made beautiful sense for business, too. Too many products were far too complicated, Robert thought. *What's elegant, what works? Sony—the simple design. The Evian bottle, for that matter. And those German kitchen appliances. It's the same idea.*

At that moment, the beluga caviar arrived. Caviar, toast, vodka. *Very simple.* Vodka. Clear, pure, the essence of liquor. *Caviar,* he thought. "Ca-vi-ar. One two three."

The printout continued:

"As a result of writing haiku, you will: be more alive to the present moment, recapture the freshness and vividness of perception you had as a youth, deepen your appreciation of nature and your place within it, and realize the potential of each moment for profound realization."

Okay, okay—enough. It was getting too touchy-feely. He understood it; he didn't need it to change his life. Besides, he was becoming interested in the business application of the idea. Simplicity. "Sim-pli-ci-ty. One two three four." No good.

He skipped ahead.

"To start writing haiku, you need only be on the lookout for a 'haiku moment' in your daily life." All right. He understood what they were getting at. Like the frog. But how to apply it to business? Without ending up with one of those hideous inspirational posters. "Soar." One. "Teamwork." Two.

"Haiku traditionally follow the seasons and include a *kigo* or season word. In Japan, there are *saijikis* or season word reference books with thousands of entries to help poets in each season as well as in the 'New Year.' While today many poems do not contain a *kigo,* knowing and using them will help you to become aware that topics for your haiku are almost inexhaustible."

The seasons. He tried to find analogies to the fiscal year. First quarter, fourth quarter. He looked for a word to evoke each of them. Nothing came to him. "An-nu-al re-port." At least it was five syllables. But it was dreadful. "Q 1 earn-ings." One two three four. Even worse.

He read on, flipping to the next section of printouts. These were about form. This was fascinating. He loved form, rules—constraints and freedom. The convention in Japanese was 5-7-5. But in English, haikus should really be shorter, because of the nature of the language. The point was economy. Maybe 3-5-3 or just short-long-short. Save the punch line. Divide it into two sections. In Japanese it's really all written as one line. Because of the way the Japanese language works, you can put the words in any order you like. You can say, "Bob gave it to the bartender," using eight different word orders. Not changing the meaning, but only the nuances. A syllable can belong to two lines at once. Like a pun. It was called *segment strapping*. All these rules.

And all fascinating stuff. That's why that badhaiku was badhaiku. They violate these rules.

Is there one right way of organizing a business, an assembly line? A universal way of doing business. Cross-cultural? Responding to human rhythms?

It turned out the rules were more flexible in English. Jack Kerouac, the Beat poet, was quoted. "I propose," he started, as though he were in a business meeting, "that the 'Western Haiku' simply say a lot in three short lines in any Western language. Above all, a Haiku must be very simple and free of all poetic trickery and make a little picture and yet be as airy and graceful as a Vivaldi Pastorella.

"In haiku it is always the same time: now; and it is always the same place: here."

Robert was itching to try one.

Okay, what to say? He wanted to write about a business concept. What about brands? He'd just been to a conference on branding, and he was still thinking about it. "Brand equity." It's real equity, but you can't put it on a balance sheet. Except in the UK, he remembered.

He turned over one of the printouts and wrote "brand equity" on the back. That was his first line. *That's five syllables. No, it's four. Poetic license,* he thought. After all, Jack Kerouac thought it was all right. Four was okay. He wanted to keep going.

"Balances books." He liked the alliteration.

And brands can balance the books; they add equity to the balance sheet. Neat. Great. How clever. He was having fun.

Brand equity
Balances books

Even more alliteration. But maybe this part should be the end lines 2 and 3. Like the punch line.

He was aware he had a form problem. How many syllables now? He didn't want to just blow it off. What if you pronounced "brand" like it had two syllables? Like you were from the Midwest? "Bra-and." "Bra - and - e - qui - ty": that makes it five. He needed seven for the second line. How about adding an "s"? "Brands"—that adds one. Not really, but close enough. He wanted to move on.

Now all he needed was a beginning. "Experience." They had talked about "experience brands" at the conference. And it created another alliteration, E(xperience) E(quities). And it had five syllables (ex-per-i-ence), no, four again.

Whatever. This was brilliant!

Experience
Brands equities
Balance books

He looked at it. It had three lines. It looked like a haiku. It had alliteration. And it was complex—it could be read in different ways. The equities of experience brands. Or experience the equities of the brands. Robert glowed with delight. He suddenly wanted to show it to Meg, or at least read it to her. He reached for the phone, then thought better of it. *It's late; she won't be there.* He thought briefly about showing it to the flight attendant. Angela. One two three.

No sooner had he thought of her than she appeared. "Sir, I noticed that you might need more paper?" He nodded. The lights were out in the cabin. She leaned in close to open the tray in front of his seat. He smelled her perfume—was it perfume or a bath lotion? The tray revealed a small drawer containing stationery, personalized with his name on it. In one continuous movement, her hands removed the paper, placed it on his writing surface, and smoothed it.

The movement of her hands, the movement of the plane. The sound of the engine. Unattached. He did not show her the poem.

He looked at it.
It had three lines.
It looked like a haiku.

EXPERIENCE
BRANDS EQUITIES
BALANCE BOOKS

On the clean sheet, he wrote out the haiku again. Done.

Exultant and exhausted, he wanted to sleep. The flight attendant cleared his tray, brought him a fluffy down comforter, and with a quick gesture transformed his seat into a bed. She turned out his overhead light.

Robert slept badly. Syllables bounced in his head, repeated themselves, transformed themselves without his permission. Unrelenting rhythms, business concepts. "Pro-cess or-i-en-ta-tion." He dreamed that he had woken up, feverish and sweating. The flight attendant appeared with a cool damp towel. "Va-lue mi-gra-tion." Gently, she removed the drops of sweat from his forehead pearl by pearl. "One-two-three-four-five." Her touch was sharp, like acupuncture needles. "To-tal qua-li-ty." He realized the touch was her long red fingernails. Suddenly someone was screaming at him, *"Where is the business plan?"*

He woke up to the captain's announcement: "Ladies and gentlemen, we will be starting our descent into the Tokyo area in fifteen minutes, and we expect to be landing at Narita Airport in one hour. We hope you have had a pleasant flight, and we look forward to serving you again."

He stirred under the comforter and slowly sat up. He was not sweating. No one was screaming. He remembered his haiku. Blinking, he sat up and looked again at the poem.

He was embarrassed. It didn't work. It lacked something. The problem wasn't the form—it was structurally correct, give or take a syllable. It even had segment strapping—not easy for a beginner. The problem was with the content, the spirit. It was not a poem. It had no soul. He thought back over the last printout he had read. The haiku moment. He had had no moment, no inspiration; it was purely an exercise in form, and an inaccurate one at that. Disconsolate, he dressed and readied for arrival.

The flight attendant brought him his jacket. Jeans & Sneakers zipped up his pack.

The 747 taxied to a halt. As the small group of travelers assembled by the aircraft door, something slipped in Robert's mind, and time stood still. A hand outside knocked on the aircraft door, and the flight attendant pulled the red door lever in a large arc to release the catch. The air didn't move—not even the air conditioning intruded on the moment. The flight crew and the ground crew exchanged polite greetings. Suspended. In a sudden strange moment, Robert saw the aircraft from the inside and the outside simultaneously—he saw himself and the people around him frozen in time. As if he had died and ascended from his body, Robert was both the perceiver and the perceived. Both A and the opposite of A. On the jetway stood a Japanese woman, formal yet gracious, her long black hair pulled up on top of her head, there to greet arriving passengers. He made eye contact, she gave him a warm smile. Now he was here. Was he here? Was it jet lag? Motionless yet moving, the flight attendant signed the ritual paperwork certifying the arrival of the flight. And his subjective experience was hers as well—shared through her behavior, not her experience. A temporary—yet eternal—space of connection between them. Noncommittal, and therefore the ultimate expression of freedom. A thank-you to existence itself.

The jetway secured, the flight attendant indicated that it was safe for him to disembark with an almost imperceptible movement of her hand; his hand twitched involuntarily in response—sensual, yet detached and floating. A moment of ultimate satisfaction, not because of its physical accomplishment but merely because of his realization of the possibility of such a moment. He looked into her eyes. They were black and infinitely deep, like a tunnel, receding infinitely.

And suddenly he heard a voice inside himself revealing it. Without a thought of form or meter or line or style or syllables or segments or alliteration, it spoke out:

Service
Being There
When Needed.

WHAT DOES THE BUSINESS PARABLE MEAN?

This business parable uses the activity of writing poetry to explore the essential nature of the customer experience. The parable introduces a dual perspective: it foregrounds the customer's subjective experience while veiling the airline's carefully planned performance. Robert's experience is seamless, but behind it lies another reality that required more effort: the company's orchestration of that experience. Robert has enjoyed unparalleled service on his flight from Los Angeles to Tokyo, and as a trained en-

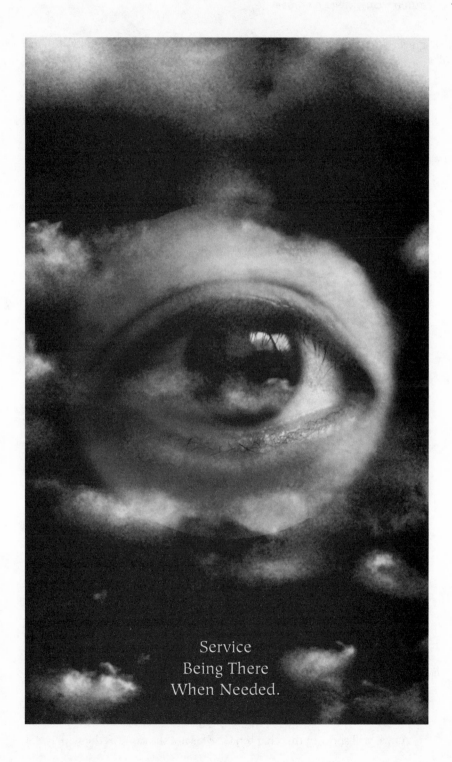

Service
Being There
When Needed.

gineer and manager, he tries to express his thoughts in the analytical *bizz* terms with which he feels most comfortable. Ultimately, though, Robert's experience is a transcendental one. The service he has enjoyed on his flight defies analysis and logical description—Robert finds that the only way to express his experience is to abandon rigid rules and analysis and open himself up to poetic expression.

Whereas experience is for the customer to savor and enjoy, it is for the organization to create and orchestrate. In other words they need customer experience management as a mastercraft to bring *bizz, buzz,* and *stuff* to any form of customer contact. This is not always easy and, as we will see, some companies show little interest in doing it.

CUSTOMER EXPERIENCE MANAGEMENT (CEM)

In his last book, *Experiential Marketing,* SCHMITT argued that traditional marketing—characterized by viewing the consumer as a rational decision maker and focusing on the features and benefits of products—was being challenged by a new marketing paradigm, which focused instead on customers' experiences, treating customers as both rational *and* emotional beings.

Since the publication of *Experiential Marketing,* this trend has exploded. Now experiential marketing is everywhere you look, and it shows every sign of accelerating and expanding. A number of companies, among them Procter & Gamble and Coca-Cola, have formed experiential marketing initiatives. Conferences on experiential marketing, experiential branding, and experiential communications are being held. Communications firms, Web design firms, and retail firms are all engaged in improving the customer experience. Forrester Research predicts that experiential marketing will become an $11 billion industry by 2003.[19]

At the same time, business organizations are undergoing a fundamental shift in the way they regard customer experiences. Managing the customer experience is no longer considered just a marketing issue: it is increasingly becoming a management issue. As SCHMITT argued in the last chapter of *Experiential Marketing,* the entire organization needs to become experience-oriented. Delivering a satisfactory customer experience requires the intelligence and resources of the whole business, under the umbrella of customer experience management (CEM).

As we will show in this chapter, CEM is not the same as the widely discussed CRM (customer relationship management). CRM is an important component of CEM, but it is far from being the whole story. In reality, CRM often amounts to nothing more than sophisticated, software-driven sales automation, whereas CEM is concerned with the total experience at any point of customer contact, before and after purchase, across the entire customer lifespan.

In this chapter, we first address the question, What are experiences? We then take a look at different aspects of CEM, including CRM, experiential communications, service performance, the customer lifespan, and the internal customer (i.e., employee) experience, which form the key tasks of this mastercraft.

WHAT ARE EXPERIENCES?

Experiences occur as a result of a customer's contact with the company in a variety of settings: in the store, at a trade show, during a sales call, during a promotion, in front of the TV, on the Web. These experiences are the perceptions of the company or brand that result from direct observation of or participation in events.

Because experiences are perceptions, they are *subjective.* In terms of creating marketing communications, the subjective world of the customer counts. What matters most is understanding how we can get a customer to have a certain experience. As a result, when it comes to the experiential aspects of management rather than its functional aspects, we need to adopt the customer's perspective.

CUSTOMER RELATIONSHIP MANAGEMENT (CRM)

From account executives to sales representatives, from telephone call reps to product managers and engineers, almost all employees interact with customers at some point or another. For years, companies have wanted CRM software that can handle all these touch points and integrate them into one database as the holy grail of what used to be called ERP (enterprise resource planning). CRM promised numerous benefits, including shorter sales cycles, integrated customer feedback, and increased loyalty. In the late nineties, this dream became a reality as several companies started to offer such software.

aspects of
customer experience management
(CEM)

customer relationship management
(CRM)

experiential communications

service performance

the customer lifespan experience

the employee experience

The term *customer relationship management* has been used in two different ways: to refer to individual customer-company contacts and to refer to the integration across different contact points. Current software (e.g., by IBM/Siebel) can handle both. Let's take a look at what's involved in these two situations.

Consider the following individual customer contact situation. A customer calls the company by phone with a complaint. The service agent who receives the call starts a call record: who called, what the problem is, which equipment or service is involved, and when the call was received. The service person then assigns a response person and specifies the time frame when the service person should respond and when the customer should be contacted by phone again. The phone system may also be linked to a field service assigned to fix the problem. In that case, the call would go into a service system so that the field engineers have the information available (preferably on a mobile device) when they fix the problem. In this case, there is a single customer touch point, despite the complexity of the task.

In contrast, a multiple-contact situation between the company and the customer occurs when the customer responds to an in-store promotion by e-mail to the company and receives a product and a follow-up questionnaire by mail. In that case there were three customer touch points: in-store, e-mail, and regular mail.

Whether individual contacts or integration across contact points is concerned, most CRM is all *bizz*—very efficient and process-oriented—but it lacks *the buzz*. It does not have to be that way. CRM tools can easily be used to create *buzz*. For example, when a service person pulls up a service menu for a customer's birthday, there should be a clear instruction about how to respond and what *stuff* to use to celebrate the occasion. On your birthday, the newspaper you subscribe to has the chance to do something special. The hotel chain that you are loyal to has the same chance. Each time SCHMITT stays in a Shangri-La Hotel in Asia on his birthday, he gets a splendid birthday cake! The trick to adding *buzz* to CRM is true personalization. Not just personalization in the sense of individual data fields integrated across platforms, but personalization with a human face—seeing the person behind the record and data field. CRM technology makes many things possible; your job is to think creatively about how to use it.

EXPERIENTIAL COMMUNICATIONS

Customer experience management is having a major impact in the communications industry. Experiential communications include all sorts of special events, from Web casts and sponsorships to unusual happenings at trade shows. For example, where once exhibition visitors expected product information, they now are being asked to immerse themselves in a branded experience.[20]

SAP, the enterprise software provider, had the image of a stodgy German engineering company with a product, R/3, that was overly complicated, difficult to install, and cumbersome to maintain. With the Internet and its new product, mysap.com, launched in 1999, and with more than a million users of the system within a few months, SAP became more like a Microsoft than a traditional enterprise applications provider.

As a result, marketing had to change. In 2000, Hasso Plattner, co-founder and co-chairman of the company, hired Marty Homlish, who had worked for years for Sony and been instrumental in the success of Playstation. As Plattner said, "I always wanted to have someone from a company with a strong brand name. There are some things a software company typically does not know. We believe if you have a good product it has to sell. Because it's obvious, it's a good product. But there is obviously much more. He has experience how to launch a product from a perception point of view."[21]

As Homlish described, he needed a dictionary to make sense of the SAP jargon and all its acronyms, and even when he understood the individual components, he still had difficulties parsing sentences. The message was too complicated and confusing to customers. The objective was to articulate clearly, simply, and consistently a *bizz* message: what SAP does—i.e., improve efficiency of people in companies and in turn the efficiencies of the companies themselves.

At the Sapphire 2000 trade conference in Las Vegas, Homlish created *the buzz:* the notion of living in a live marketplace. The center of the convention floor in the Venetian Hotel was a Sony-style 360-degree-surround theater. The theater show engaged the senses, with huge screens and surround-sound stereo. Inside the open-structure auditorium, an actor (dressed in high-tech material jumpsuit and sneakers) interacted with video on a large screen and provided narration onstage. The Story: How mysap.com integrates all business applications, illustrated via the histories of four young business people succeeding in the snowboarding business through collaboration. The show was subsequently taken on the road to four cities.

Immediately surrounding the theater were booths demonstrating the key components of mysap.com, giving one-minute snippets of marketplace, business-to-business procurement, enterprise resource planning, and the other components. From the central theater branched several avenues where Internet solutions were demonstrated. The avenues ended in plazas that provided areas spacious enough to hold 1,500 people, and were stocked continuously with food for refreshments. The idea was to give customers a unique convention experience.

The SAP case illustrates that even trade shows can be fun. Next time you attend one, notice how much attention the driving ranges, the fashion shows, and the food lanes in front of the trade booths attract.

SERVICE PERFORMANCE

Unfortunately, not all customer experiences are so satisfying. Poor service can be one of the most nerve-racking experiences that consumers endure. Consider the following true story.

The New PDA: A Consumer's Nightmare

12/18/99	SCHMITT hears of a new Palm-compatible PDA, and excitedly tells David Rogers, the Associate Director of the Center of Global Brand Leadership that he directs, about it. David tries to order one through the Web site, which states it will take six to eight weeks! He calls the phone order number; after thirty-five minutes on hold, he's again told three to four weeks.
12/19/99	Schmitt orders new PDA.
1/15/00	The PDA arrives.
1/19/00	The PDA's battery cover is poorly attached; SCHMITT has to tape it up and realizes the stylus is also easy to lose.
1/20/00	Schmitt calls & orders a new PDA cover & 5 styluses.
2/1/00	Schmitt calls to check on the order and is told they should arrive by February 15.
2/22/00	The tape fails, and the batteries fall out of SCHMITT's PDA on a business trip and he loses all the information saved in it. He is not able to reload it until returning to NYC.
2/28/00	David calls on SCHMITT's behalf, to check on his parts order, explaining that it was supposed to be here two weeks ago. Lisa answers, sees the order on file, and says it's coming. David asks to speak to a supervisor and is transferred to Gillian. Gillian says, "Yes, we have your order. I don't know why it hasn't gone out! We have them in stock." David explains the recent loss of memory due to the batteries falling out, and says the order is needed urgently; he requests that it be sent out express mail. Gillian says she will put an URGENT note on the file,

and it'll be processed now. She says they can send it out FedEx: "It should be there in one to two days, but it'll definitely be there in five business days."

3/6/00   No sign of stylus and battery cover.

David calls in the morning. Christine answers, says she sees the order in SCHMITT's file "for one battery cover and two styluses." "That's supposed to be five styluses," David says. "Oh yes, I'm sorry, it does say five styluses," she says. David asks to see if it says when the order is going out. She says, "Well, I can't call that up. You see, these aren't in the system like a purchase order, so there's no invoice attached to them. I just have a note of your request here on the computer under SCHMITT's name." David asks to speak to Gillian. She is not there. He asks to speak to another supervisor, is put on hold, then cut off after waiting five minutes.

David calls back, is put through to supervisor Barry. Barry says, "The person who handles these orders for parts is not in right now, but she'll be in later. Why don't you try back this afternoon." David explains that SCHMITT is leaving for a long trip to China at the end of the week, and he needs the parts by then, to avoid having the batteries fall out again and losing all the data. Barry says to "call back in the afternoon."

David calls back at 4:30 p.m., and asks to speak to Barry. After a long hold, he's told secondhand that Barry says, "The person handling these orders is now in, and just starting to *process* the requests which have been waiting on her desk. He'll have to call back tomorrow to check on status; they should go out by the *end* of this week." David asks that a message be given to Barry to make sure that SCHMITT's order is given priority status, because he needs it to *arrive* this week before he leaves for China and because his order is so overdue.

3/7/00   David calls again, asking for Barry. Again, he waits on hold while a long message is taken from Barry, who evidently doesn't wish to speak with him. The message is that "the orders for parts have all been processed now, and Schmitt's own parts are packaged in a box, going out, and will arrive by end of the week." David asks for the FedEx tracking number so that he can contact FedEx and be sure the box reaches SCHMITT's hands before he leaves the country on Friday. He is told that "FedEx doesn't pick their boxes up until the afternoon. The box is actually still waiting in a stack of boxes, but you can call back in the morning to get the tracking number."

3/8/00   David calls in the morning, asking for the tracking number. A woman on the phone says, "Oh yes, I see your order under 'Schmitt,' for a battery cover and two styluses." "It's supposed to be five styluses!" David says. "Oh, okay." He asks to speak to Barry, who is out for two days, in meetings. He asks to speak to Gillian—she isn't in today. He asks to speak to any supervisor. After a hold, Shauna comes on the line. She says that she's seen SCHMITT's file, and the parts are on back order. David says he was told that they had been boxed up yesterday to go out FedEx. "No, there's a note here that we have your request, but the parts are back-ordered. It couldn't be going out, because we don't have any parts. But as soon as they get in, your order will be processed." When should David call back to see if the parts are in? "Try back in a week."

NOTE: There is no phone number to dial to order parts from the PDA maker. And when you dial their customer service line, your *first* option given is to press "1" if you wish to check on the status of an order for a PDA "placed before Nov. 25" (at this point, orders placed more than fourteen weeks earlier).

• • •

In late March, two battery covers finally arrive, but no styluses. At this point, two new problems have surfaced: the batteries still read at 75 percent when they run out of energy, causing the unit to stop working; and when the PDA crashes, its restart button does not work. Therefore, one can only restart it by removing the batteries and losing all the information within. This happens twice to SCHMITT while he is traveling in China on business in April.

In late April, SCHMITT brings his PDA in to the final meeting of his class on "Managing Brands: Identity and Experiences." Having related this unfolding saga in class throughout the course of the semester as an example of brand management for a new product competing in a new technology market, he boxes up the PDA and sends it to the chairman, with a letter from the students thanking him for providing such an enlightening case study in service mismanagement.

Does the chairman respond? What do you think?

This sad tale leaves us with some lessons. In The Garage, service provides a great experience if it follows three general principles. Service must be:

- *Prompt:* Time is of the essence in many service situations; customers usually want the product, the repair, the missing component *now,* not later
- *Competent:* The service personnel must be able to handle the service request. This is not just a matter of knowledge and training but of having the right technology (database, supply-chain management system, and fulfillment system; see Chapter 4).
- *Responsive:* The service personnel must take the customer's perspective, empathize, and be responsive. In a complaint situation, customers may be upset; thus, service personnel need training in handling feelings and emotions

These three rules make up professional service handling. They are *the bizz* of service management.

But there's also *the buzz.* And *the buzz* makes a great service a performance. *Buzz* service is a dance; it is choreographed. It is often unobtrusive, because it goes with the flow and anticipates things. You can tell that *buzz* service people love their jobs; they have fun.

W, the hotel chain discussed in Chapter 1, provides that sort of service. Singapore Airlines has done so for many years. The Citibank ATM machine does, even though it is automated. The layout of the ATM screen is perfect: well lit, well organized. You interact directly with the screen, not with buttons placed ambiguously next to it. The integration between text, visuals, and sound works well (all the way up to the distinctive *hissing* sound the machine makes to draw your attention to the receipt). That *hiss* is *buzz*.

Think back for a moment to the business parable at the beginning of the chapter, in which Robert receives perfect service and is hardly aware of it:

Service
Being There
When Needed.

Buzz service is service as a haiku moment.

CUSTOMER LIFESPAN

Let's first look at a small but significant incidence of customer lifespan mismanagement.

It's Saturday evening. There is a package to be sent urgently to Hong Kong. SCHMITT is in a big rush to make it just in time to his local overnight delivery drop-off station. He makes it—at 6:58 p.m. But the door is closed. He gestures to the service people inside to tell them that it's not quite 7:00 p.m. and begs them through gestures to open the door. They don't. At that very moment, one of the drivers slips out of the side door and heads for the truck. (You know, these are the friendly types out of the commercials and business case books that make sure that you absolutely, positively get your stuff delivered wherever you want it at any time.) SCHMITT politely says, "Sir, I understand this facility is closed. Is there another one still open?" He gets a brisk no for an answer. He continues, "This is extremely urgent. Do you know any other provider that's still open?" The service person laughs and raises his voice. "Why should I tell you anything about our competitors?"

Here is why:

Because I have about 5,000 personal and business friends around the world in my Palm Pilot and because I can e-mail them with the click of a button and tell them what outrageous treatment I have received, and ask them to pass along the story.

Because I own a small business and have your company as the key service provider and have spent tens of thousands of dollars with your company.

Because I am a shareholder: I have owned stock in your company for three years and have bought more stock each year.

Because if you do, I will be thankful forever, and tell everyone the story, and that will get you lots of new customers.

Because I will feature the story in my next book and in the dozens and dozens of speeches I give each year to thousands and thousands of business people.

Because I can put your company on one of the Internet complaint sites, and trust me, my story with me barely making it is as good a story as your commercials about the heroic acts of your service people.

Because you are not just a deliveryman but also a nice guy who helps people in need.

Because it's just not such a big deal, and I may thank you.

Because it's actually faster and easier than being nasty.

Because it is silly to hold people hostage to your proprietary knowledge.

That's why.

Do you remember the classic black and white film *Miracle on 34th Street?* It's one of those standbys that are shown on TV every Christmas time. The story involves Santa Claus—the *real* Santa Claus, not an actor—taking a holiday job at Macy's as . . . Santa Claus. When a store manager overhears the jolly old elf telling a shopper that they have just what she's looking for at rival store Gimbel's, he is outraged. But then Macy's management catches on. Serve the customer. If you don't have what the customer needs, find out who does and let the customer know. You may lose this sale but you gain the customer's goodwill, which will last long after she's forgotten what she was looking for on this shopping trip. In the movie, Macy's embraces this policy. Not to be outdone, so does Gimbel's. Warm and fuzzy? Sure. But ultimately everyone benefits, especially the consumers.

It all comes down to management over time. The customer experience must be managed across the entire customer lifespan. Loyal customers are preferable to a constantly changing customer base. Loyal customers are easier to service. They typically buy more over time. They recommend the company to others. They save the company the acquisition costs of new customers in the form of advertising costs, new sales calls, and promotional offers. So, isn't it then worthwhile to do a little extra once in a while? To surprise customers and delight them with something creative?

Customer lifespan management can learn a lot from another "lifespan" field, a field within developmental psychology that deals with human lifespan development. As lifespan developmental psychologists have shown, throughout a person's life there is a series of "critical events" that can leave deep scars or have very positive impact for things to come in the future. Such events include toilet training, the first few days at school, adolescence, college graduation, the first job, the first child, the second wife (or husband), midlife crisis, retirement, and so on.

There are similar "critical events" in customer lifespan management; the only difference is that they are usually much easier to manage. In fact, in some cases the customer may not even recognize these critical events, but through your initiative you can create special moments in the "lives" of your customers. And then celebrate them to the customer's delight. Such events include the first contact between the customer and the company, the first purchase, the anniversary of the first purchase, a complaint, the first recommendation, upgrading, and volume purchases. It is up to you to help define the defining moments of the customer lifespan.

THE EMPLOYEE EXPERIENCE

Finally, managing the internal customer experience is just as important as the external customer experience, especially in a service business—that is, in two thirds of all businesses in the United States. Companies are doing poorly at it. What destroys the experience? Well, lots of things. For example:

- Hierarchies
- Bad offices (with poor lighting, ugly framed mission statements, outdated computers and software, windows that don't open)
- Motivational blah-blah PR
- A sense of entitlement, arrogance, and lack of humor
- Patronizing corporate training programs
- Stupid, endless meetings
- Silly approval processes administered by sadistic bureaucrats

And companies are extremely unoriginal in orchestrating celebrations of valuable employees. How valuable do you really feel, for example, when:

- You win the "employee-of-the-month" award, but the employee-of-the-month award gets rotated until everyone's been famous once
- You get a gift that just promotes the company (how many key rings and tote bags with the company logo on them do you really need?)
- Your boss takes you to a restaurant where you would not want to go if you'd been asked (and you'll have no drinks because the accounting department won't reimburse for that)

Companies need to show more originality in rewarding employees. Three simple rules:

- Employees are asked and can decide. This rule applies to the design of their offices and office equipment, the choice of meetings, and the types of celebration gifts they'd like to receive
- Employees are treated as individuals (even within a team). No unnecessary defaults or general approval processes
- Employee experience management must be done from the employee's perspective, not the company's. Save the blah-blah PR for the outside; on the inside acknowledge with pride, but don't brag.

Managing the employee experience is also a matter of mastercrafting technology, as we have seen already in chapter 4. Instead of hindering communications with noncompatible systems and complicated technologies, how about taking advantage of the latest in Web-enabled communications? Avaya, the former Enterprise Networks Group of Lucent Technologies, is an example of a company that has excelled in this field. A U.S. and worldwide market leader in sales of messaging and structured cabling systems and voice communication and calling center systems, Avaya provides customer relations management systems to businesses where the "customer" is often the employee.

Avaya's approach consists of "breaking down barriers that come between people, networks, and systems": reducing the complexity of interactions and enabling compatibility of different technologies. Avaya provides customers with a wide array of easy-to-use online tools and services, of course; but customer experience is enhanced not only by the opportunity to choose among these tools and services but also by interactive systems, including self-service systems that allow customers to investigate and resolve support issues themselves, as well as access new product information and training-related material.

Bringing an old system into a new era of technology, Avaya has taken the lead in providing e-business innovation to call centers, those crucial front lines in customer experience management. By integrating communications within task-handling processes, connecting call center agents to a company's customer data reserves, Avaya's systems open the way for efficient and intelligent customer service, the kind of contact that allows and encourages employees to actualize their potential, and—not coincidentally—builds employee loyalty.

If companies worked even a fraction as hard to please their employees as to please their customers, the workplace would provide an entirely different experience. But it's not just a metaphor. In a very real sense, your employees are your customers. Recall the situation in "Category Killer," the business parable that introduces chapter 4. In the story, it's evident that the company's marketing is missing its target audience: the young and the wired. At the same time, the company's pathetic use of technology and its slowness to change represents a real obstacle for employees trying to get their work done. Both perspectives come together in the person of the killer temp. Your employees represent a tremendous resource—a firsthand connection with the world outside. Don't ignore them.

SUMMARY

Mastercraft—even handcraft—the experience!

chaos and the dancing star

"The Sleeping Beauty of the Corporate World"

Once upon a time, in an economy far, far away, there lived a gentle and handsome CEO with his wise Chairwoman. Though they worked together extremely well, they were sad because they had no successor.

Then one day, when the Chairwoman was walking through the forest near the corporate headquarters, a little bird flew up to her and alit on her shoulder. Whispering in her ear, the little bird told her that soon a successor would appear who would become both CEO and Chairwoman, and who would quadruple the company's market cap in the future.

The CEO and the Chairwoman were overjoyed, and when the successor showed up at the headquarters, the whole company celebrated. They held a wonderful ball to celebrate her arrival. And among the guests were the board members of the corporation. Each board member brought a wonderful gift for her. One gave her the gift of managerial decision making, another the gift of emotional intelligence. From other board members came the gifts of fiscal responsibility, strategic thinking, and killer stock options.

Then suddenly there was a terrible noise, and an evil board member, who had not been invited to the ball, stormed into the headquarters. Enraged at having been overlooked, this board member said to the CEO and Chairwoman, "I, too, have a gift for your successor. I will return the kindness you have shown me. My gift is this: soon after your successor has assumed power, she will prick herself on the pin of a nametag and die— and with her, the entire corporation." And then the evil board member departed as quickly as he had appeared.

Then all the guests wept and moaned that the successor would die so young. But there was one more board member left to bestow her gift on the newcomer. "I cannot entirely undo the curse the evil board member has laid," she said, "but I can change it. The successor will not die, but rather fall into a deep sleep—and with her, our entire corporation—until a prince from a far economy shall awaken her with a kiss."

As time went on, the successor showed all of the gifts the good board members had given her, and she did her work with great wisdom. And the CEO and Chairwoman ordered that all nametags for corporate events be the sticky kind, not the kind with pins, to prevent the terrible curse from coming true.

One day, not long before she was set to assume leadership of the company, the successor was walking alone in the forest outside the corporate gates. And there she met a traveling office supplies vendor, a funny little man carrying a satchel on his back. Seeing the successor, he opened his satchel and began showing her his best-selling items, among them a nametag with a pin on the back. "What an efficient product," said the successor, who had never before seen such a tag. "These are reusable and do not say 'hello my name is.'" And in reaching for the shiny bauble, the successor pricked her finger.

Suddenly she began to feel drowsy. Lying down on the ground, she felt one part of her body after another becoming numb and falling asleep. First her thighs became heavy and fell asleep, and the company's facilities began to shut down. Then her hands fell asleep, and all the company's machines ceased to function. As the drowsiness spread across her breasts, the finances of the company deteriorated—cash flow became negative and liabilities increased. Then the feeling reached her forehead, and the company's strategy became stagnant: no new corporate initiatives could be launched. Finally, her eyes became heavy, and the company's marketing and communications fell still.

Not just the successor, but also the CEO and the Chairwoman and all their management team, and even the division heads, fell into a deep and dreamless sleep.

And around the bower where the successor lay sleeping grew up a lush, thick netting of bureaucracy, hiding and sheltering her sleeping form. The support staff came each day to the sleeping successor, and reported to her that the company had not launched a creative product in a long time and that they were rapidly losing market share, but still she slept and would not wake. Even when she was shown that there were thousands of customer e-mails accumulated in the Inbox, she did not stir from her deep slumber.

There she remained for many quarters.

Industry leaders from economies far and wide, as well as venture capitalists with their legal staffs, heard the tale of the sleeping beauty of the corporate world, and bid to be the one to awaken her with a kiss and/or a hostile takeover. But none could get through the bower of bureaucracy. The thicket trapped them and they gave up, scarred by the experience.

Until one day a prince from a far-off economy—some said he was an incarnation of the Management Guru—came to the little industrial park in the shadow of the corporate headquarters.

And he said to himself, "I know I can find a way to awaken the sleeping beauty of the corporate world."

When the Prince approached the thicket of bureaucracy, he saw the scarred faces of the wheeler-dealers and their attorneys, but he was not afraid. He strode confidently to the thicket, and the bureaucracy parted before him, and the Prince entered. So tightly did the bureaucracy grow together that the bower was very dark, and the prince could hardly see. But not far in front of him he saw the golden tresses of the successor shining in the dim light.

The ground was wet from a recent rain, and the footing was muddy. The Prince approached the sleeping beauty and knelt on the ground beside her. Gently, he began to push the mud off her body. Leaning down over her softly breathing form, he kissed her warm, pink thighs. She stirred, and immediately the company's facilities sprang back to life. The Prince took up her lily-white hand in his own, and kissed it, and the company's operations and machines began to run. The Prince next kissed the soft and fragrant breasts, and the company's finances turned around. Gently brushing the mud from her face, the Prince bent down and kissed her clear, white forehead. Suddenly the company's strategy was awake and alive again with creativity. Next he kissed her sleeping eyes, and the company's marketing and communications revived. Finally, the Prince kissed the ruby lips of the successor, and she awoke.

"Who is the hero who has awakened me?" she asked. And at that very moment she glimpsed the nametag on his lapel, its pin gleaming in the soft light, and it said "Prince of Creativity."

UNLEASHING YOUR ORGANIZATION'S HIDDEN CREATIVITY

So the Prince of Creativity comes along and awakens the sleeping corporate beauty with a kiss. Unfortunately, it isn't that easy. As we have shown in this book, building The Garage and unleashing a company's hidden creativity is a more complicated process. Broadly speaking, this process includes the following three steps:

Step 1: Aligning the bizz, the buzz, *and* the stuff *at the organizational level.*

As we saw in Chapter 2, to be a garage an organization needs to bring together *the bizz, the buzz,* and *the stuff.* Otherwise, the organization does not use and leverage creativity in an optimal fashion. Moreover, nurturing the positive tension between *the bizz* and *the buzz* is crucial because it is the management of this tension that transforms chaos into creative outcomes. To achieve these objectives, an organization must be properly aligned for corporate creativity. As Chapter 3 showed, this alignment requires that the key decision makers of the organization make creativity a top priority; that they set up a garage structurally; and that they recruit creative talent with various skills.

three steps in managing corporate creativity

step 1:
aligning *the bizz, the buzz,*
and *the stuff* at the
organizational level

step 2:
infusing creativity
into projects and initiatives

step 3:
applying the mastercrafts

utilizing technology
leveraging the brand
creating the experience

Step 2: Infusing creativity into projects and initiatives

Creativity must not only be managed at the macro level of the organization, it must also be infused into specific projects and initiatives at all levels. In other words, creativity must become part of daily work, part of the everyday planning and decision-making processes of the organization. The second part of Chapter 3 provided a set of working and communication tools to help individuals and teams within an organization to harness creativity. In addition, resource tools for managing the creative tension between *the bizz* and *the buzz* offer techniques for exploring creative solutions.

Step 3: Applying the Mastercrafts

Finally, we need to use technology, branding, and customer experience management—in every individual project and in all parts of the creative initiative across the organization. In Chapters 4–6, we explored the Mastercrafts of The Garage. We demonstrated how each Mastercraft must be creatively managed in its own right, a task that calls for applying the Blueprint and the Toolbox. Once properly managed, these Mastercrafts can in turn foster creative initiatives at the macro and micro level.

In addition, The Garage presents an opportunity to rethink the purely rational and analytical concepts of traditional management that we alluded to in chapter 1. We believe that today's business environment requires a new understanding of traditional management concepts. Let's look at some examples.

MISSION AS INFORMED DIRECTION

We'll start with the concept of the mission statement, every company's self-declared attitude toward itself and the world around it. A "mission statement" is supposed to give the organization's direction and specify its core values and overall purpose. Organizations everywhere devote tremendous energy to pinpointing and publicizing their missions. Yet in traditional management most mission and vision statements are very similar and regurgitate trivialities like "Our mission is to become the world's leading supplier of XXX. We want customers to be successful because their success is our success. Our ultimate purpose is to deliver quality products and value, and to add value for our shareholders."

What exactly does all this mean? It's vague, it's general, it doesn't really say anything special about the company. Your high school English teacher wouldn't let you get away with something like this. What's more, most mission statements seem to be little more than foregone conclusions, put together so that employees can say, "Yep, we do that. We're succeeding; we're accomplishing our mission." Mission statements may change over time, but it's usually only to accommodate the latest business terminology. What a waste of time!

In The Garage, only real progress counts—not the illusion of progress. Rather than deciding on how to structure actions based on vague, static mission statements, employees in The Garage should use a company's mission to provide *informed direction. Bizz*-wise, informed direction is based on the best possible information about the marketplace, about technology, and about customers. The Garage then uses this information to create direction. "Where do you want to go today?"—the Microsoft slogan from the late nineties—is the dictum of informed direction. The point of informed direction is not to respond opportunistically to environmental change; the point is rather to stay in touch with the things going on all around. The *buzz* of informed direction comes from responding to ongoing changes in information. Informed direction doesn't hang in a frame on the wall; it is a living, breathing, dynamic process for guiding an organization.

STRATEGY AS STRUCTURED OPPORTUNITY

In traditional management theory, "strategy" refers to setting objectives and examining choices. Often the word is mindlessly added to other business terms, resulting in phrases like "the strategic view of customers," "the strategic perspective on competition," or "looking at value strategically," which sound pretty good but mean very little.

There is another, more substantive problem with the traditional concept of strategy. A company's "core strategy" focuses on achieving long-term goals, and the lifespan of such goals may be as long as five to ten years. However, the pace of change in business has become extremely rapid. In the face of such quick change, long-term goals are beginning to look irrelevant, and long-term planning seems more and more like a silly indulgence rather than a sensible approach to business.

What's the alternative to the traditional view of strategy? It is to think about strategy as *structured opportunities*. A company needs to have some way of assessing the environment and setting goals. Rather than developing a long-term, inflexible, step-by-step strategy, we suggest that companies think in terms of an interaction of planning and action. By analyzing the environment on an ongoing basis, businesses can detect a structure. Within this greater structure, opportunities present themselves. The more creative a company can be in scanning the environment, the more opportunities it will find.

The risk of such a near-term focus is that a business may fall prey to opportunism. To avoid this hazard, businesses need to have a system in place to explore trends. Environmental scanning systems can be developed to identify and evaluate opportunities. Special teams, made up of senior management and functional experts in different business areas, can scan the market and propose and evaluate opportunities. For example, an opportunity for a brand extension would be evaluated by a team of branding people and senior managers. Potential mergers would be examined by senior managers and finance people. Company teams thus become like SWAT teams that constantly scan the environment for opportunities. To take full advantage of opportunities that arise, businesses also need to have a quick decision-making process in place. In this environment, waiting too long can mean missing the boat.

COMPETENCE AS A FLEXIBLE STRENGTH

In traditional business, management competence is often viewed statically. Something the organization knows. What it is good at. Its skills and capabilities. In today's environment, such a static view can mean death. As Clayton Christensen, a professor at the Harvard Business School, has shown in his book *The Innovator's Dilemma,* many successful companies and erstwhile technology leaders often fail against new technologies precisely because they focus on their core competencies.[22] "Old soldiers never die," as Douglas MacArthur said, "they just fade away."

Today's environment requires companies to display *flexible strengths* rather than fixed competencies. Flexible strength combines the best of *bizz* and *buzz.* Strength is a *bizz* concept, implying the ability to withstand stress and to perform exceptionally well in a particular area. The *buzz* of flexibility promises openness and spontaneous tractability. The result is an organization that is prepared to use its existing strengths in new and original ways. Flexible strength may mean leveraging core competencies in new industries. Out of this grows the attitude of taking on challenges and overcoming obstacles.

IMPLEMENTATION AS PEAK PERFORMANCE

In traditional management, "implementation" is supposed to be the tangible culmination of strategy and competence, accomplished through scrupulous dedication and hard work. Unfortunately, most implementation in business is hardly of that nature. Implementation is traditionally a process that follows the military model—once the strategy is established, the troops follow it. As long as the troops have been properly drilled, all they have to do is march; motivation is unimportant. As a result, implementation is often more like following the drum and cutting corners when the drummer isn't watching. The military model works well among highly disciplined people, trained to operate in a very hierarchical structure, under the severe threat of losing their lives, their friends, their homes—in other words, the stakes are about as high as they ever get in life. Despite the popularity of war metaphors in business writing, most employees do not feel such pressure every day from nine to five. Nor should they. When business is portrayed as a constant life-and-death battle, some employees are bound to think their bosses are crying wolf. Thus, implementation is rarely carried out in the soldierlike fashion that business leaders would wish.

In The Garage, mechanical implementation is underperformance. Instead, the goal is *peak performance* that surpasses even imagined goals. The metaphor here comes from sports, not war, and we think it is more appropriate. The world of sports provides inspiration for performance in The Garage. Athletes discipline and prepare themselves through regular physical and mental training. They understand that they don't have to win the big game every day. At the same time, they understand that every day's training is an essential part of the whole. They look forward to the key moments when their skills will be tested. In The Garage, employees are like athletes: well trained and well versed in *the bizz,* and *buzzing* with excitement to see the outcome of their work. When the moment comes to show their skills to the utmost, they are prepared to give a peak performance. They never lose sight of the larger goal, and they understand how the day-to-day contributes to it. And if one approach does not work, they pick themselves up and try again.

EMPOWERMENT AS INDEPENDENT INITIATIVE

"Empowerment" is another core concept of traditional management. Since its invention, it has been associated with the notion of helping individuals achieve self-actualization. Typical empowerment techniques include showing sincere appreciation to employees, sharing information, and setting clear criteria and standards. Although these communication tools make sense, they are always viewed from the perspective of the boss, who controls the amount of self-determination each employee will be allowed. There is always a corporate hierarchy in the background, and the notion of "empowerment" takes on an almost patronizing tone. Empowerment is like letting a child go to the store by itself but not giving it enough money to make the experience a meaningful exercise in character—not allowing it to make judgments on its own. By and large, corporations that "empower" their people still don't really entrust them with anything very important.

Independent initiative is quite different from empowerment. Like the athletes discussed above, team members in The Garage take real responsibility for what they do. They may have coaches helping them along, but ultimately it is their initiative and talent that are tested. For example, The Garage's nonhierarchical structure could mean that team leaders change from project to project and they may be higher or lower in rank. The project leader drives the project along but is critically dependent on the team members' independent initiative.

CONCLUSION

The Garage presents a new way of thinking about business—thinking that moves away from the purely mechanical, hierarchical, and analytical model of business that underlies traditional management. A business that is not just managed by rational objectives. A business that focuses on direction, opportunities, and flexibility. A business that focuses on peak moments and initiatives. A business that gives birth to a dancing star out of chaos.

NOTES

1. David Pilling, "Big pharma sees the beauty of thinking small," *Financial Times,* Monday, April 2, 2001, p. 10.
2. Edward Luce and Louise Kehoe, "Cisco finds itself victim of its past successes," *Financial Times,* Wednesday, April 4, 2001, p. 23.
3. Alan Robinson and Sam Stern, *Corporate Creativity: How Innovation and Improvement Actually Happen.* San Francisco: Berrett-Koehler Publishers, 1998.
4. This case is based on the following sources, among others: www.americanexpress.com; "AmEx Holds Contest for Budding Blue Card Developers," *Business and Industry* (July 2000), p. 12; "American Express Launches 'Code Blue,'" *PR Newswire,* June 6, 2000; Miriam Souccar, "AmEx Contest Pitches Blue to Web Start-Ups," *American Banker,* May 17, 2000, p. 13; "Blue Heading Toward 2 Million Mark," *Business and Industry,* March 20, 2000, p. 2.
5. This case is based on the following sources, among others: Nick Raio, "The Waiting Is Over: Starwood Rolls Out W New York Hotel," *Hotel Business,* January 17–20, 1999; www.whotels.com; and several articles on *PR Newswire.*

6. This case is based on the following sources, among others: Erick Schonfeld, "NTT DoCoMo," *e-company* (August 2000), p. 76; www.nttdocomo,co.jp; Miki Tanikawa, "Phone Surfing for a Few Yen," *New York Times,* August 19, 2000, p. 35; "NTT DoCoMo I-mode Subscribers Top 10 Million," *Japan Economic Newswire,* August 7, 2000.

7. This case is based on the following sources, among others: www.hp.com; Elizabeth Corcoran, "The E Gang," *Forbes,* July 24, 2000, p. 78; Patricia Sellers, "The 50 Most Powerful Women in Business," *Fortune,* October 16, 2000, pp. 130, 138.

8. Interview with Haruki Murakami on www.salon.com.

9. Gary Hamel, *Leading the Revolution.* Cambridge: Harvard Business Press, 2000.

10. "Gates Unveils Internet-based Programme," *The Irish Times,* June 23, 2000, p. 51.

11. Cable News Network Financial, Entrepreneurs Only, May 25, 2000, transcript #00052504FN-118.

12. Scott Kirsner, "Collision Course," *Fast Company* (January–February 2000), pp. 118–44.

13. Rem Koolhaas, *S, M, L, XL.* New York: Monacelli Press, 1995.

14. See Mary Modahl, *Now or Never: How Companies Must Change Today to Win the Battle for Internet Consumers.* New York: HarperCollins, 2000.

15. *Vogue* (January 2000).

16. www.interbrand.com.

17. Chris Macrae, *Brand Chartering Handbook: How Brand Organizations Learn Living Scripts.* New York: Addison-Wesley, 1996; Alan Mitchell, "Out of the Shadows," *Journal of Marketing Management,* 15 (1999), pp. 25–42.

18. Naomi Klein, *No Logo: Taking Aim at the Brand Bullies.* New York: Picador, 1999, p. 131.

19. "The Next Step for Brands on the Web," *Business Wire,* March 20, 2000.

20. Charlotte Goddard, "Brands Make a Stand," *Marketing,* January 14, 1999, pp. 25–26.

21. Hasso Plattner, keynote speech, SAP Sapphire Conference, Las Vegas, June 14, 2000.

22. Clayton Christensen, *The Innovator's Dilemma.* Boston: Harvard Business School Press, 1997.

INDEX

horror, and love story genres. SCHMITT THEATER has staged the world premiere of the corporate opera "Der Turm von Babble, Inc." at IBM Headquarters; produced the modern dance "The Historical Progression of Business: A Dionysian Extravaganza" at Columbia Business School; and created "The Monolith"—a conceptual art piece that made an appearance in the Whitney Museum's collection of twentieth-century art on February 24, 2001, from 2:00 to 3:30 P.M. SCHMITT FASHION markets and distributes experiential body art and collaborated with runway models, photographers, and designer Jungeun Lee's "La Va Woman" brand on an interactive fashion event on corporate identity. For more information on these and other ventures, contact **www.meetschmitt.com.**

Laura Brown is a writer and business communication consultant based in New York City. She has ghostwritten business books on subjects ranging from Chinese business to e-commerce design to venture capital, and she worked with Schmitt on *Experiential Marketing: How to Get Customers to SENSE, FEEL, THINK, ACT, and RELATE to Your Company and Brands* (in which she also appears as a mystery character . . .). She consults with corporate clients on a wide variety of marketing and communication issues. Her clients have included AOL Time Warner, CitiGroup, Interbrand, The Wharton School, and TMP Worldwide. She also serves as a Senior Program Developer on a curriculum of Web-based business communication courses for Columbia Interactive, Columbia University's online learning initiative.

Laura Brown was born in California and received a B.A. in English from UCLA. She holds an M.A. in Drama from the University of London and a Ph.D. in English and Comparative Literature from Columbia University.

ABOUT THE AUTHORS

SCHMITT (a.k.a. Bernd H. Schmitt, Ph.D.) is one of the most creative and original business thinkers today. Known globally as a brilliant speaker, consultant, provocateur, and iconoclast, SCHMITT is transforming the business world's understanding of strategy, creativity, and innovation.

SCHMITT is Professor of Business at Columbia Business School in New York and the Executive Director of the Center on Global Brand Leadership. He is the author of *Experiential Marketing: How to Get Customers to SENSE, FEEL, THINK, ACT and RELATE to Your Company and Brands* (The Free Press, 1999) and co-author of *Marketing Aesthetics: The Strategic Management of Brands, Identity and Image* (The Free Press, 1997).

SCHMITT consults and gives keynote speeches for companies around the world on corporate creativity, strategy, branding, and experiential marketing. Moreover, he has launched several groundbreaking ventures, which are shaking up the business world. SCHMITT CINEMA has produced films and movie trailers about business using the documentary,